COACHING THE FRONTLINERS

THE COMPLETE GUIDE TO COACHING THE OFFENSIVE LINE

Harold Etheridge
United States Military Academy

COACHES CHOICE™

ISBN: 1-58518-415-2
Library of Congress Catalog Card Number: 2001090984

Book Design: Jeanne Hamilton
Diagrams: Jeanne Hamilton
Cover Design: Paul Lewis

Coaches Choice
P.O. Box 1828
Monterey, CA 93942
www.coacheschoice.com

DEDICATION

This book is dedicated to all the offensive linemen, past and present, that have played for me and given their loyalty and dedication to this great game. I salute these young men and thank them for their commitment, and all they've given to me as their coach.

THE DOCTOR

ACKNOWLEDGMENTS

Much of the credit for this book must go to my wife, Jeanne. Her patience and encouragement over the several years of this project have made it all possible. Behind every successful football coach is a great family. In Jeanne, Clayton and Eliza, I am fortunate to have the very best.

A special thanks to Earl Browning, for providing the idea and initial motivation in getting me started on this project.

Thank you to Coach Steve Farmer for his countless hours of administrative assistance.

CONTENTS

CONTENTS

Chapter

FOREWORDS

I was excited when Harold told me he was writing a book. I have watched Harold coach for many years and admire his skill as a teacher of offensive line play.

Coaching the Frontliners is a comprehensive resource that:

1. Thoroughly analyzes multiple blocking techniques and fundamentals.
2. Offers approaches to an array of topics such as game planning, practice organization, communication, alignments, blocking schemes, and calls.
3. Discusses motivation as it applies to linemen and coaches.
4. Presents drills for developing fundamental habits.

I am sure that you will enjoy *Coaching the Frontliners.* It is the most current and extensive manuscript of offensive line play that I have seen.

Paul Alexander
Offensive Line Coach
Cincinnati Bengals

Coach Etheridge is one of the finest technician coaches in the country. His concepts are revolutionary and have helped strengthen and enhance our offense over the years. I have been astounded at the skills that our young linemen achieve as he continues to accelerate their learning curve. His book is a must read for coaches at all levels who are thirsting for the "cutting edge" approaches that lead to victories.

Todd Berry
Head Football Coach
United States Military Academy

INTRODUCTION

I've been blessed to coach for over two decades, both at the high school and college level. I'd also like to extend a great deal of thanks to the head coaches I have worked under in the past and present, Alex McAlister, Ron Madrick, Jerry Claiborne, Bill Curry, Jim Heacock, and Todd Berry. All have had tremendous influences on my life, both personally and professionally. My development as a coach is a compilation of what I have learned from each of these great men. My love for the game has been, and always will be, with the big fellas up front. Let's face it, these guys are not the best athletes on the field. If they were, they'd be on the other side of the ball. What makes my job the most rewarding is that I have the opportunity to develop and bring along young men who may have less talent and ability, but have the heart and determination to be good at what they do. I'll take those two ingredients over talent and ability any day.

To play on the offensive line, it takes courage, dedication, loyalty, and a burning desire to excel. I want the "want-to guys" playing in my unit.

Therefore, this book will cover a wide range of topics that I feel are the foundations of being an offensive line coach and will include materials that I have put together or picked up from some of my mentors throughout my coaching career. I hope that after reading this book, every coach will come away with some ideas that will help his team and players reach their potential on and off the field.

SECTION I

GENERAL TOPICS

OFFENSIVE LINE PHILOSOPHY

OFFENSIVE LINE CREED

THE OFFENSIVE LINE COACH

EVALUATING OFFENSIVE LINEMEN

TEACHING PROCEDURES

PLANNING YOUR PRACTICE

DEVISING THE GAME PLAN

GAME PLANNING PROTECTIONS

ANALYZING YOUR OPPONENT

EVALUATING GAME-DAY PERFORMANCE

GUIDELINES FOR PERFORMING DRILLS

CONDITIONING OFFENSIVE LINEMEN

LONG-SNAPPING TECHNIQUES

CHAPTER 1

OFFENSIVE LINE PHILOSOPHY

Offensive linemen need body control, balance, quickness, agility, and strength in order to block effectively and to protect the passer. They must learn to recognize defenses and adjust their blocking scheme accordingly. They should get off on the snap count and react to the defender's reaction, so that they can sustain their blocks and defeat the defender one-on-one. Offensive line play is nothing more than a proper first step, hat placement, striking ability, maintaining leverage and getting movement.

As coaches, we should incorporate a sound and simple scheme that allows the players to master the techniques and fundamentals of their position (i.e., know who they're blocking and how to do it). It is simple "hat-on-hat" with all-out effort and execution from snap to whistle. The players need to know and understand their assignments and blocking techniques, and that they are accountable.

As coaches, we sometimes get too caught up in X's and O's and forget the players. We get caught up in doing too much, and before long, we're not good at anything. To me, it's simple. We should reduce the number of schemes, and not spend a lot of time on assignments or rules that will come with front recognition. As a coach, I spend time helping my players understand the concept of the play, the scheme used on the play, and the blocking techniques and tempo. I use the pyramid theory with my guys so they understand what the play is designed to do. We then focus on what their blocking assignment is, what techniques will be used, and the tempo of the scheme being used (examples of schemes, zone counter, draws, etc.).

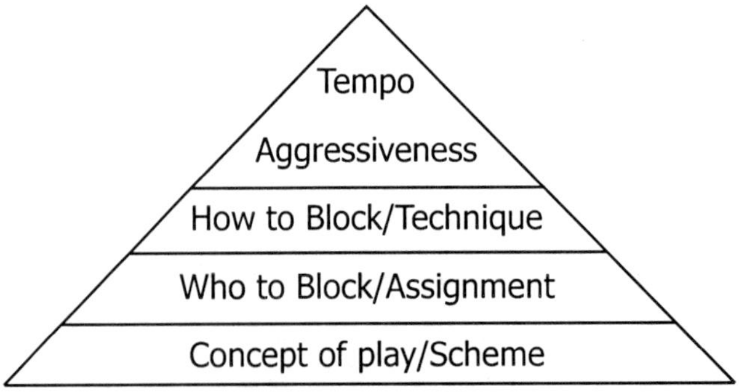

CHAPTER 2

OFFENSIVE LINE CREED

You are involved in a game that requires explosiveness, movement, and leverage. You are a proud member of an elite group due to the very nature of this game. It is competitive, intense, brutal, combating and exhausting in both a physical and mental sense. Many are called, few are chosen, and even fewer excel at the game.

Life on the O-line is similar to life. We have structured the game where goals are clearly defined and achieved only through teamwork. Play outside the rules, and you're penalized. Carelessness will lead to mistakes and, ultimately, to defeat. We work with a deadline and limited time-outs. You knock them down, and sometimes you get knocked down. It's getting back up that is the measuring stick of a man's determination.

Honor this great game, and it will provide you with riches, both emotional and tangible. Cheat this game, and it will break you and humble you in a heartbeat. The choice lies in your mind and in your heart. This is the difference between winning and losing.

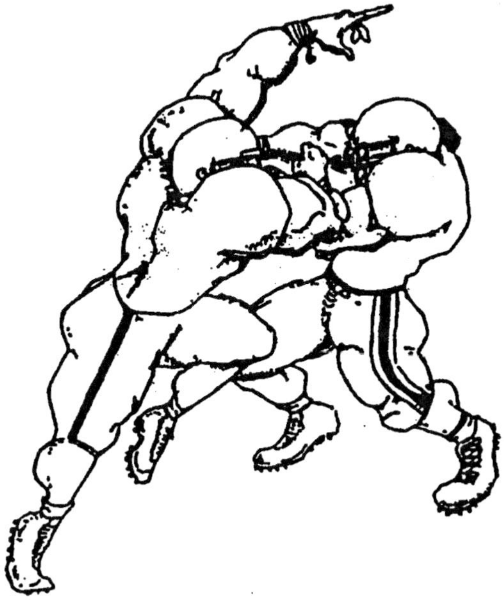

CHAPTER 3

THE OFFENSIVE LINE COACH

To develop an offensive lineman into a good football player, I believe, as a coach, you have to be a great teacher. Be yourself. Coach your style, not someone else's. I've always believed that players are a reflection of their coach. Take pride in your job. You owe it to these young men to never shortchange the ones you serve.

As a coach, you should not assume that your players already know everything they need to know, regardless of their playing experience. It should be a goal of the coach to help the player understand the basics of the concept of the play, his role, the blocking scheme, and the techniques involved to execute the play.

It's not only our job, but our responsibility, to give our players every chance and tool available to develop them into the best players they can be. In simple terms, we must attempt to take our players where they can't take themselves, both on and off the field. Get to know your players. Your involvement has got to be more than just football. You've got to have personal involvement with each individual so they know you're interested in them. Each player should feel that you are extremely supportive and that they can trust you. There's a saying, "Treat a person as he is, and he will remain as he is. Treat a person as if he were what he could be and should be, and he will become what he could and should be." If you treat people as they *could* be for long enough and are truly sincere about it, then more often than not, that's what you'll get in return. By providing a positive influence, your players will become closer to attaining their goals than they would have otherwise. Every coach should create an environment where each team member feels good about himself. If the coach can stay upbeat and positive, then everyone feels like a winner. A positive attitude is contagious.

How do you put everyone in the unit in an environment that allows them to be the best they can be?

- Give the players responsibility for their various roles. They should know that if they don't get it done, the job won't get done. When they do succeed, they've accomplished something important.
- Be personally involved with each individual, in a positive way, that will let the players know you're interested in them and are totally supportive and loyal.
- Give your players guidance to make good decisions.

The most effective way to teach is through a combination of positive reinforcement and fear. You've got to be able to control your personality to get the optimal response from the players. A coach needs to be sufficiently strong mentally in order to determine how positive, how sincere, and how negative to be. How, where, and when should you jump a player's case? That depends on the individual. You have to know your player well enough to determine how, where, and when it's time to push the "punish" button.

The more positive statements you can make, the more you will be able to help get your players out of the quicksand. Tell them how good they can be, but also what it's going to take to achieve their goals. Each player has to face reality (i.e., here's where you are and here's where you're going). The players are the ones who have to look in the mirror each day and know whether they have done it the right way. Players must develop a sense of pride. It takes discipline, dedication, and a sense of pride to excel. "Don't be a retriever, be an achiever" are words to put in practice.

Almost anything that the human mind conceives can be profitable, but only if you believe in yourself and work at a championship level.

C – haracter

H – eart

A – chiever

M – ental toughness

P – ride

IMPORTANT COMPONENTS TO THE COACH/ATHLETE RELATIONSHIP

LOYALTY — To understand who we are; to give without expectation of return; to say and do what we believe and mean it. The key factors in this regard are family, togetherness, and unconditional love.

FOCUS — To clearly focus on the task at hand, whatever it takes to get the job done.

COMMUNICATION — To deal with players honestly and sincerely; to treat each player as an individual; to be a good listener.

BUILD CONFIDENCE — To reward players with praise and encouragement, letting them know when they've done something right or wrong (on and off the field).

BUILD ONENESS — To instill unity, trust, faith, and pride.

QUALITY REPS AND DRILLS — To achieve results; nothing else is acceptable.

TEACHER — To be organized and in control; do not shortchange the players you are serving.

CHAPTER 4

EVALUATING OFFENSIVE LINEMEN

Assessing the abilities and skills of an interior lineman is one of the most important aspects of an offensive line coach's job. Many coaches don't fully realize the capabilities of their players. Many times, determinations and selections are made solely on a prospect's height, weight, speed, and on his estimated potential as a football player.

There are all types of offensive linemen — short, big, bulky, tall, rangy, and athletic. To determine what type of lineman you need, you must first determine your type of offensive style and philosophy. This step will determine what type of personnel you'll need to have a productive offense. For example, if your line prospects are bulky and lack speed, you will probably find it difficult to employ a pulling scheme in your offense. These players may make it necessary to employ a straight-ahead, power-type of offensive attack. If you can base your scheme on the type of personnel that you have, it will give them a chance to be successful. It's that simple.

As stated earlier, interior line prospects need body control, balance, quickness, agility, and strength in order to block effectively and to protect the passer. The progress that is made in developing the linemen's potential, improving their skills and techniques, and molding them into a cohesive unit will determine whether the running back can get the football beyond the line of scrimmage, or the quarterback will have time to set up to throw downfield. It is difficult to move the football with any consistency if a team does not have sound blocking schemes and techniques.

An offensive linemen must learn to recognize defenses and adjust their blocking schemes and techniques accordingly. It is important that they get off on the football, and respond appropriately to the defender's reaction, so that they can maintain and finish their block. A player's skill will limit the extent of the offense. In order to be a pulling team, your guards must be able to pull and trap, and pull and lead on sweeps, counters, options, and bootlegs. If your interior personnel cannot execute these skills, you may have the plays in your coaches' playbook, but you would be kidding yourself and shortchanging your players to include them in your game plan.

QUALITIES OF THE POSITION

TOUGHNESS: Mentally and physically.

FEET: Footwork, foot speed, and pulling ability.

FLEXIBILITY: Power producing angles; Z's in the knees; bent-knee player.

QUICKNESS: Initial start, reaction, and adjustment.

BODY CONTROL: Balance and ability to play in space.

LEVERAGE: Body-on-body; play pad-under-pad.

EXPLOSIVENESS: Quick get off with the first step.

CONTACT: Hand placement, blow delivery, and upper body violence.

FOLLOW THROUGH: Over a wide base and the ability to finish.

STRENGTH: Functional strength to get it done.

Among the ways to evaluate your personnel for the various positions on the offensive line are the following:

1. Evaluate his speed with regard to initial change, agility, quickness, coordination, and reaction qualities, and playing in space.
2. Assess his blocking agility – Does he have a good initial change? Is he a good position blocker?
3. Does he keep his feet and maintain contact?
4. Does he take pride in defeating his opponent?
5. Evaluate his ability at level one blocking, route to linebackers, trap blocking, down field blocking, and protecting the passer.
6. Can he pull and trap, pull and lead interference, and complete his block?
7. Has he been successful to this point in his playing career primarily because of his size and strength?
8. Can he play better on the left or right side of the line?

Because the offensive center is the key offensive lineman, it is not a position to be filled as a last resort. He is the leader of the pack and the director of the offensive line. A prospect should not be assigned to play offensive center because he is too slow to play anywhere else. This is a mistake commonly made by inexperienced coaches. Your center controls the timing of your offense. Therefore, he should be one of, if not your best athlete. If your center does not execute the center/quarteback exchange properly, he will cause the team's offense to falter because of fumbles, miscues, and poorly timed plays. Since the center/quarterback exchange is frequently the cause of fumbles, the reasons for ball-exchange miscues will be reviewed later in this book. The center must also be able to make the shotgun snap in addition to executing the basic fundamentals and techniques of the other interior linemen.

Among the factors that can be employed to evaluate your player personnel for the center position are the following:

- Can he snap the football?
- Can he shotgun snap the ball consistently?
- Is he agile enough to pull out of the line and pick up an outside blitzer on pass protection?
- Can he man block a defender in a one-on-one situation?
- Is he agile enough to get to the second level to block or cut off a linebacker?
- Does he have the same abilities as the other offensive linemen?

The following offensive-line checklist can help you rate your personnel. Assigning points (i.e., 5-outstanding, 4-above average, 3-average, 2-below average, 1-poor) to specific criteria can provide you with a rating scale that can help you determine what your player's or prospect's strengths and weaknesses are.

-Quickness off the ball

-Body control

-Agility and balance

-One-on-one blocking

-Blow delivery (run)

-Sustain block

-Finish block

-Reactions/adjustments

-Route to linebackers

-Speed for position

-Pulling ability, trap

-Pulling ability, lead

-Downfield blocking

-Aggressive and reckless

-Second effort, desire

-Pass sets

-Blow delivery (pass)

-Pass blocking

-Upper body strength

-Lower body strength

As a coach, it can be demanding and time consuming to evaluate personnel. However, it is necessary and one of the most important things you do as a coach. You should ask yourself where each player can be put by position to do the best job possible for your offense. You can drill the players to evaluate their abilities. It then becomes your job to place each player in his best position.

To find a good solid football player, ask yourself whether he has the following attributes.

- Does he have good athletic ability?
- Does he have a great attitude?

- Does he have a good work ethic?
- What is his family background?
- Does he have good character?
- Can he be trusted?
- Is he tough?
- Does he love the game?
- Does he understand football?
- Does he have academic intelligence or football intelligence (or both)?

CHAPTER 5

TEACHING PROCEDURES

As a coach, the classroom should be your most valuable teaching tool. This is where you can make the game of football an educational experience. The classroom is where a coach can give his players the opportunities to learn and see situations so they can understand and experience the basic blocking fundamentals on a sound progressive basis. In this environment, they can understand the concepts and mechanics of blocking techniques, and learn how to carry out assignments and adjustments.

It's your job, as a teacher and coach, to never assume a player knows more than he does, even if he is an experienced player. There's an old saying — "what you know is simple, what you don't know is difficult." The same holds true for offensive linemen. It's not only the right thing to do, but it's your job and responsibility to give each player every opportunity to learn and grow. Remember, "coaching is teaching — teaching is coaching."

The following coaching points are not only important for effective teaching, but also true for proper player execution and performance:

- First things first – it is important to start from the beginning and build a good foundation.
- Football is a game of "repetition" – do it over and over.
- Football is a game of "habit" – conditioned reflexes.
- Teaching and coaching is a big package – have a plan with good breakdown progression.
- Follow the winning edge: simplicity, consistency, and stability.
- Coach your personality – not someone else's.
- Motivate your players – don't sit around on your butt.
- Give quality coaching – you're asking for quality.

- Know what you're coaching – if you don't know, FIND OUT!
- Look for and recognize your mistakes in coaching.
- Be a coach, not only on the field, but also off the field.
- It's not what you know, but what you teach – be sound and simple.
- Believe in what you are coaching.
- A confused player won't perform well on game day.
- Coach the intangibles – the winning edge: discipline, commitment, enthusiasm, effort, and pride.
- Football is a game of demands and confrontation. Require each player to perform and do it right; confront the player when he is wrong.
- Linemen must be taught to recognize and adjust to blocking situations.
- The coach who permits a player to practice doing something wrong all week has lost an opportunity for a player to get better or improve his ability.
- The coach must have the ability to sustain practice and be energetic.
- Too many coaches are not trying to be good coaches and don't give enough effort. We ask our players to give effort, the same holds true for coaches. Remember your players are a reflection of their coach. They wear your colors.

There are many teaching tools you can use as a teacher, for example, chalkboards – scheme assignments, tip sheets, blocking sheets, scouting reports, written tests, teaching tapes, drill tapes, practice tapes, and game tapes. Have a plan for each daily classroom session outlining what you need to get across to your players. Be organized, prepared, and thorough when you begin each session. Your players can be motivated by selling them the plan. To be successful, *every member* of the unit must believe in and understand the plan. In the first meeting each year, the following fundamental precept should be stressed to the players: "If you do the things we teach you to do, we will be successful." This is a challenge to the players and it is repeated periodically.

There's a saying in football – "Go over all the 'what ifs' so that they do not become 'if onlys'." Take each play, technique, or drill and break it down so your players understand what the play is designed to do, what their blocking assignment is, and what technique will be used to allow them to master the fundamentals of their position.

As a coach, your goal should be to take this broad concept and turn it into something to which every player can relate. Remember, we're all creatures of habits with different learning styles. As a result, you need to be creative and to respond to each player's unique teaching needs as required. Try to take your players where they can't take themselves. I feel this is the real challenge of coaching and provides a tremendous motivation.

Among the additional elements that are essential factors in classroom teaching that you should require are promptness, attentiveness, and proper dress. Furthermore, involve your players in the teaching process by challenging someone every day on the blackboard. Let them teach you in order to find out what they know. When reviewing film, let them explain their mistakes, techniques, assignment, etc. Have specific objectives for each meeting. When using tape to teach, make sure your visual aids are ready to go prior to the meeting. Don't waste time cueing up the tape. Remember that time is valuable. Also, cover your daily practice schedule with your players so they will know what is coming and what will be expected of each practice segment. Be sure you give your players time to get from meetings to the practice field. Lastly, be yourself, upbeat, and positive, and have fun with your team.

IN-SEASON WEEKLY MEETING SCHEDULE

SUNDAY	Grade film, review film – note general problems and make corrections, introduce and review next opponent.
MONDAY	Players day off – coaches game plan.
TUESDAY	Cover scouting report, base looks, stunts, blitzes, installation, and game plan. Review opponent's best game; hand out blocking sheets.
WEDNESDAY	Review Tuesday practice; make corrections; review cut-ups of opponent (stunts/blitz/GL-SY).
THURSDAY	Review Wednesday practice; make corrections; review opponent's worst game to pump up your unit.
FRIDAY	Play the game; written test; tip sheets; review Thursday practice; give them challenges to go after.
SATURDAY	Cover key points; chair drill or walk through; final reminder.

DAILY PROCEDURES AND OBJECTIVES

Our basic approach is to out-execute and out-work our opponents. Among the procedures and objectives on which we put a daily emphasis are the following:

OFFENSIVE LINE PROCEDURE

- BE ON TIME – NO EXCUSES
- BRING REQUIRED MATERIAL
- SIT BY POSITION AND DEPTH CHART
- BE PREPARED TO TEACH UNIT ON BOARD

- WATCH FILM – PRACTICE/DRILLS/GAMES
- STATE OF MENTAL READINESS – FOCUS
- CORRECTIONS/INSTALLATION
- PAY ATTENTION TO DETAIL

OFFENSIVE LINE OBJECTIVES

- KNOW YOUR BUSINESS – ASSIGNMENT – EXECUTION
- MENTAL AND PHYSICAL TOUGH UNIT
- MASTER YOUR FUNDAMENTALS AND TECHNIQUES
- BLOCK WITH AN ATTITUDE – KILLER INSTINCT
- PROTECT YOUR QB – WHATEVER IT TAKES
- COMPETE – ALL OUT EFFORT – SNAP TO WHISTLE
- UNIT PRIDE – DESIRE AND PRIDE TO BE THE BEST
- KNOWLEDGE OF SCHEME AND CONCEPT OF PLAYS
- DEVELOP AND MAINTAIN CONSISTENCY
- NO EXCUSES – GET THE JOB DONE

OFFENSIVE LINE PRACTICE PROCEDURE

- COME READY TO WORK: CONCENTRATE; FOCUS ON TASK AT HAND
- PRACTICE "GAME LIKE" — ALL OUT EFFORT – COMPETE – "SNAP TO WHISTLE!"
- BE INTENSE – FUNCTION AT MAXIMUM EFFICIENCY
- EXECUTION – ACCOUNTABILITY – KNOW YOUR BUSINESS
- STRIVE TO IMPROVE YOUR GAME DAILY
- MASTER YOUR FUNDAMENTALS AND TECHNIQUES
- QUALITY REPS – SELF DISCIPLINE
- MENTAL AND PHYSICAL TOUGHNESS
- WILLING TO PAY THE PRICE – WHATEVER IT TAKES – GIVE IT UP TO YOUR COACH
- PERSONAL PRIDE AND DEDICATION TO BE THE BEST

CHAPTER 6

PLANNING YOUR PRACTICE

Coaching is not easy. Time is of the essence. Therefore, your practice schedule and plans should be well thought out and organized in order to be effective. As you know, "coaching is a race against time," and "time lost on the practice field is never given back." This chapter reviews the factors that are vital in planning, organizing, and conducting practice sessions during the season in order to accomplish your objectives. Regardless of the level of competition, the following suggestions and guidelines on practice planning should prove to be helpful. You should spend considerable time and give ample thought to your practice plan and stick to it. Your plan should be detailed for every practice segment and situation. You will obtain the best results if you put your plans down on paper. Situations often arise during the course of practice that cause a coach to be hurried, and consequently, make him forget to cover something. To help you avoid this situation, keep a checklist that includes all the various phases of football that you need to cover. Build your checklist around the offensive schemes, drills and fundamental techniques involved to ensure you're preparing your players to be successful. A typical football practice schedule may be divided into five segments: pre-practice, specialty, individual, group-combo, and team periods.

PRE-PRACTICE PERIODS

This time segment can be employed as a recognition or walk-through period. You can review different types of situations — base runs, protections, special plays, screens, draws, and reverses versus your opponent's fronts and adjustments. This segment can be used as a mental time for your unit to step through and rehearse their assignments according to defensive fronts. This will enable you to determine if your players have retained their assignments from the meeting room to the practice field.

SPECIALTY PERIOD

This segment of practice is devoted to the kicking game. Since most offensive lineman are not involved in the kicking game, you can use it as valuable time for specific work with your unit. You could employ this time as a warm-up period, using drills for agility and reaction. You could also work on pulling, trapping or whatever other phases of line play you usually don't have a lot of time to cover in your individual periods.

INDIVIDUAL PERIODS

During this part of practice, the focus is on individual fundamentals and techniques. Time management is critical. As a coach, you must select drills that will teach and develop the particular fundamentals and techniques that you think will help your team. These drills should be identified prior to the start of the season so that you are organized, prepared, and thorough. The selection of drills and the amount of time devoted to them should be decided by looking at the purpose of each drill and asking yourself, "How much are we going to utilize what this drill teaches in a game, skill, fundamental, technique or segment of the game?" In order to answer this question, a coach must determine if the drills relate to the techniques and schemes being used offensively. Remember, it's the little things that are important. Don't try to do to much. Individual drills should attempt to teach the following:

- To teach coordination of eye, mind, and body.
- To develop confidence and poise.
- To evaluate and align personnel.
- To improve fundamentals, skills, and techniques.
- To create game-like situations in practice.
- To practice the way you are going to play the game.

The drills you select should fit your objectives, methods, and philosophy of coaching football. You should include drills that will thoroughly cover all the essentials of your offensive scheme.

GROUP-COMBO PERIODS

This segment of time is devoted to different units going against each other. These periods can be used as a time to hook up with the defensive line, linebackers, running backs, or a combination of all three groups. Various situations can be covered in this segment, ranging from one-on-one, two-on-two, three-on-three, half-line, full line, covering inside, and the perimeter running game. Blitz pick-up, twist pick-up and pass protection can also be performed during this period. This process gives your unit a clear view of the overall picture and still enables you to concentrate on an individual player within your unit or the entire unit.

TEAM PERIODS

The final segment is when the emphasis is placed on developing the team as a whole unit. This step is necessary in order to polish the timing of plays, to check offensive assignments, and to put the players into game situations. This will demonstrate if the players and the unit are able to make use of the techniques and fundamentals learned in practice and utilize them in game situations. The objective is the all around development of the offensive unit learning to work together.

SUMMARY

In summary, you should spend considerable time and thought on your practice plan, and all the basics of the game. It's not always the system or plays that win games, but players who execute the fundamentals better than the opposition. It is not necessarily how much you teach your players, but how effectively you teach them. Select practical and effective drills that will develop individual and unit fundamentals, techniques, and skills under game conditions. Using these sound principles should prove beneficial in obtaining desirable results.

CHAPTER 7

DEVISING THE GAME PLAN

When preparing a game plan, your coaching staff must establish it around your overall philosophy. Basically, the coaches devise a particular game plan using one of three approaches:

- A conservative-field approach, choosing a ball-control approach that relies a little more on establishing the running game.
- A wide-open offense, where you're willing to take chances and push the ball down field vertically.
- A middle-of-the-road approach being a combination of the two. In devising your offensive game plan, consider how and where your team is best able to move the football and put points on the scoreboard.

By the use of competent scouting and film breakdowns, a coaching staff can determine a profile of the strengths and weaknesses of the opponent. Your team's strengths and weaknesses should be matched up against the strengths and weaknesses of your opponent in order to give you the best chance of winning.

THE RUNNING ATTACK

To establish the running attack, you must determine whether your team can run the ball inside, outside, or both. You should devise a plan that is simple, physical, and one that moves the chains. As a coaching staff, you must take great pride in the preparation and the selling of the plan to your players. They've got to believe in the plan you want them to prepare for and execute.

It is essential to analyze and assess your opponent's defense. There are five areas of review in preparing your weekly game plan:

- Opponent's statistics
- Opponent's defensive concept and structure
- Opponent's personnel
- Basic game plan questions
- Practice format

OPPONENT'S STATISTICS

As you study your opponent, you will gain insight into the personality of the defense you're going to face. Define their strengths and weaknesses against the run and the pass, and then set your goals so it's a challenge to both the staff and the players. It's vital that your players thoroughly understand what the opponent is known for defensively. These statistics also assist the staff in making decisions concerning practice organization and how to handle specific situational emphasis. The following statistical defensive categories listed can give you insight into what type of defense you are up against:

- Scoring defense
- Total defense
- Rush defense
- Pass defense
- Average per rush
- Average per pass
- Rushing touchdowns
- First downs per game
- Third down defense
- Passing touchdowns
- Quarterback sacks
- Take aways (turnovers)
- Tackles for a loss (T. F. L.)

OPPONENT'S DEFENSIVE CONCEPT AND STRUCTURE

What are the basic fronts and structures of the defense. You should determine their base front and how many other fronts they use in different field positions and in down-and-distance situations. What type of defensive alignments do they line up in?

- Even front
- Odd front
- Gap front
- Field eagle (reduction)
- Bound eagle (reduction)
- Eight-man (4-4, 5-3, 6-2)
- 4-3 stack
- Pro 4-3
- Bear defense
- Multiple defense
- Situational defense
- Nickel defense
- Nose-man front (on center)
- Uncovered nose-man fronts (off center)

You should also identify the basic characteristics of their defense, for example:

- Attacking front
- Read front
- Stunt front
- Stemming front
- Dog: inside/out single linebacker
- Blitz: inside/out move then one linebacker
- Combination blitz
- Alignments: loose, tight, normal, flexed
- Coverage: man, zone, both, disguise
- Adjustment: motion, shifts, tight end trade

Furthermore, you need to determine their best situational defense in the following field situations, and when do they change:

- Third-down and long
- Backed-up
- Red-zone (+20)
- Short-yardage
- Goal-line
- Nickel (2-minute defense)
- 2-point play defense

You should also evaluate your opponent in the following areas (i.e., what are their strengths and weaknesses):

- Team Speed
- Team Quickness
- Strength
- Physicalness
- Tackling Ability
- Cover ability
- Closure to the ball
- Reaction to sudden change
- Reaction to big play
- Separation from blocks

Finally, you should determine your opponent's defensive tendencies relative to the following factors:

- Down-and-distance
- Field position
- Base formations
- Adjustments vs. shift, motions, trades

OPPONENT'S PERSONNEL

Analyzing your opponent's personnel can help you find ways to get the football to your best players. Try to utilize your offensive strengths and blockers to attack the defense's weakest segment. In that regard, you should determine the following:

- Three best defensive players
- Best defensive lineman
- Best inside linebacker
- Best outside linebacker
- Best pass rusher. What are his best moves, and how can we neutralize his strengths?
- Strongest level of personnel: DL-LB-DB
- Key back-ups
- Key situational substitutes: short-yardage, nickel, goal-line
- Best match ups (do they flip-flop their personnel)
- Unusual keys and tip-offs they show
- How does each position play against the run and pass?

BASIC GAME-PLAN QUESTIONS TO COVER

- What should we run and how?
- Where should we run and why?
- Where should we not run and why?
- What formations, shifts, motions, and trades dictate the defense we want to run against?
- What are our run downs?
- What are our pass downs?
- What can we expect in crucial field situations?
- How many times will we rush the ball?
- How many runs will be directed one way or both ways?
- How many practice repetitions do we need for each run?
- What is the distribution of inside, outside or off tackle runs?
- What is the distribution of fullback to tailback runs?

- How many one back runs do we want?
- How many tight end and split side runs do we want?
- What field position runs do we want to feature?
  - √ Hash-mark/upright to field runs
  - √ Hash-mark/upright to boundary runs
  - √ Middle of the field runs
  - √ Coming out runs
- What automatics do we want to carry?
  - √ Check-with-me package
  - √ Run automatics package
  - √ Blitz checks package
  - √ Unusual alignments automatics
- What additional runs/specials do we want to run?
  - √ Complimentary run
  - √ Misdirection and counters
  - √ Option
  - √ Draw
  - √ Reverses
- What runs do we want to feature in crucial situations?
  - √ Short yardage
  - √ Coming Out
  - √ Red-zone
  - √ Goal-line
  - √ 2-minute (no huddle)
  - √ Stall offense
  - √ 2-point play

PRACTICE FORMAT

Since the NCAA restricts Division I football teams to 20 hours of practice per week and the actual game counts as three hours, that leaves you with 17 hours. It is vital, then, to utilize your time effectively to establish your running attack. Each practice day should have a specific emphasis. I try to commit a total of 45 minutes per day to our run game in either a group or team emphasis. The only difference to our base schedule is that of Thursday's practice; we list the total number of plays, as opposed to the total number of periods and minutes. Our basic weekly schedule is as follows:

Monday:	No practice – players' day off
Tuesday:	Base run: as group (15 minutes)
	Base run: inside drill (10 minutes)
	Perimeter runs (10 minutes)
	Goal-line/short yardage runs (10 minutes)
Wednesday:	Base run: as group (10 minutes)
	Base run: inside drill (10 minutes)
	Perimeter runs (10 minutes)
	Special runs: draws/reverses (10 minutes)
Thursday:	Scripted plays
	Coming-out runs (4 plays)
	Formation runs (12 plays)
	Red-zone runs (6 plays)
	Short-yardage runs (4 plays)
	Specials draws/reverses (4 plays)

CONCLUSION

These categories, evaluations, and questions should enhance your ability to make sound decisions in your game planning. It is important that your players gain confidence through the coach's preparation in the meeting room and on the practice field. As a result, the players have a good understanding of what to expect in specific situations and can anticipate making adjustments more readily. You will find that your players will perform better in crucial situations when they have experienced it during the week of practice. By having your players mentally prepared, they will be more likely to execute physically without any hesitation. Preparation and communication are the basis for a positive working relationship that breeds success.

CHAPTER 8

GAME PLANNING PROTECTIONS

When planning the passing game, your coaching staff should avoid getting carried away with strategy and tactics, while forgetting to spend time teaching and drilling the basics. The plan will only be successful if your team is fundamentally sound and can execute the offense. In an effort to establish a passing attack, you must determine whether your team can complete passes in front of secondary defenders in the flats, over linebackers, or deep against the secondary defenders by particular receivers.

As discussed earlier, you must answer the following questions concerning your basic game plan in order to determine whether you are going to pass short, medium, and/or deep, or a combination of the three:

- Do you utilize play-action, sprint-out, semi-sprint, or drop back passes: three- five- and seven-step drop?
- What can you do to ensure the best protections vs. the opponent?
    - √ Primary (base) protections
    - √ Secondary protection
- What is your opposition's pass-rush ratio?
- What is their base front?
- Who are their best pass rushers? (Rate them)
- Are they a zone-blitz team?
- Do they dog/blitz often? Tendencies? On what downs do they come and how often?

- Do they utilize man-to-man or zone coverage?
- How do they adjust to shifts, motions, or trade when changing formations?
- Are they predictable on their down-and-distance tendencies?
- Do they cheat their alignments to show blitz or bait you?
- Do they disguise their dog/blitzes?
- What are the weak links in their defensive levels?
- What field-position passes do you want to feature?
  - √ Open-field
  - √ Coming-out
  - √ Red-zone
  - √ Vs. blitz
  - √ Third-down situations (short, medium, long)
  - √ 2-minute offense
- Do you want to direct the protection to or away from their best rusher?
- Do you need to use a max protection?
- Can you anticipate fronts by formation to dictate what protections to use?
- What pass-rush techniques do you have to defend?
  - √ Speed rush
  - √ Rip rush
  - √ Swim rush
  - √ Bull rush
  - √ Inside/out moves
  - √ Outside/in moves
  - √ Combination rushes
- What specials do you want to carry?
  - √. Misdirection
  - √ Play-action
  - √ Throwbacks
  - √ Reverse passes

PRACTICE FORMAT

- Review base protections strong and weak
- Blitz review all protections vs. favorite blitzes
- Twist pick-up

CONCLUSION

The method of protection selected must be simple to execute. Your unit must understand its strengths and weaknesses. You must always be cognizant of the time constraints involved in coaching. It is better to master a few protections and do them well, than attempt to do too many, and not master any. Limit your protections so you have the time to teach them well. Your players will know how and why the protections are executed, thereby allowing you, as the coach, time to perfect the techniques involved.

CHAPTER 9

ANALYZING YOUR OPPONENT

SCOUTING REPORT

Your scouting report on your opponent should be basic, short and to the point. The actual length of the report should be no longer than four to five pages. It should be informative and easy to read. As a rule, the report should cover the following topics:

Page one: defensive depth chart of personnel including, name, jersey number, height, weight, and classification.

Page two: your opponent's top defensive fronts and alignments.

Page three: your opponent's favorite twists and stunts.

Page four: your opponent's favorite dogs and blitzes.

Page five: short-yardage and goal-line fronts.

The initial scouting report is merely an orientation for your players and shouldn't be a dissertation. You should take ten to fifteen minutes during your first team meeting of the week to cover it. It is not important to give the players all of the opponent's defensive tendencies by formation, field position, and down-and-distance; they simply will not remember it all. You should prepare them throughout the week for your opponent's tendencies as you implement your offensive game plan.

FILM STUDY

As a coach, you should encourage your players to come in on their free time to study and watch their weekly opponent on film. This step will help them in their weekly preparation. Have the film you want them to watch available and an opponent film-study form that they can complete as they review the film. This will help you as a coach, knowing that they have familiarized themselves with and learned something about their opponent. By using this process, I feel it puts me, as a coach, and my players ahead of the game, making our meeting and practice time more productive.

OL OPPONENT FILM ANALYSIS STUDY FORM

Name: ____

Game Watched: ____________________________________

Review the game, then answer and fill in the questions below.

1. List numbers of defensive personnel

   Defensive line Linebackers

   Left DE #_______ Sam #_______

   Tackle #_______ Mike #_______

   Nose #_______ Will #_______

   Right DE #_______

2. Who is their best defensive lineman? _____ Why? _______________
3. Who is their best linebacker? _____ Why? _______________
4. List their top three defensive front:
   - ______________________
   - ______________________
   - ______________________
5. List their top three favorite line stunts:
   - ______________________
   - ______________________
   - ______________________
6. List their top three favorite dogs/blitzes:
   - ______________________
   - ______________________
   - ______________________

7. Do they stem their defensive fronts?YES–NO. If yes, from______to______
8. Do they tip when stunting? YES–NO. If yes, how? ____________________

   ____

9. Do they disguise or show when blitzing? YES – NO. If yes, how_______

   ____

10. Who is their best pass rusher?#_____________

    Why? ____
11. Who is their best linebacker?#_________

    Why? ____
12. Do they flip flop their defensive line? YES — NO
13. Do they flip flop their linebackers? YES — NO
14. What is their defensive-front philosophy?
    - Play loose and read
    - Play tight and attack
    - Slant/angle front
15. What front do you expect on third-and-long? ________________
16. What front do you expect in the red zone? _________________
17. Do they like to blitz in the red zone? ______________________
18. What is their strength defensively? _________________________________

    ____

19. What will it take to beat this team? _________________________________

    ____

20. List your goals for this game: _____________________________________

    ____

    ____

    ____

CHAPTER 10

EVALUATING GAME-DAY PERFORMANCE

I believe very strongly in evaluating each player's performance. Some coaches view films in a rapid manner, and their players have very little feedback on how they performed or were graded. As a coach, I believe it is vital that each scrimmage and game film be evaluated to grade your players individually and as a whole unit. This step allows a coach to determine what must be emphasized, corrected, practiced and coached prior to the next game.

Game films should be used to grade execution and to evaluate the offensive schemes and techniques the players were asked to execute. Grading helps to determine if the players know the responsibilities and techniques needed to play their position properly.

If an offensive blocker continues to make mental mistakes, he simply cannot play for you, despite the fact he is a good blocker. Mental mistakes will disrupt an offense, freeing up defensive players to make big plays that may stop an offensive drive or create a turnover.

As a position coach, you should give your players goals they can shoot for individually and as a unit. For example, you could grade such skills as: dominates his opponent, pancake blocks, pass protection shut out, M.A.B. plays (make-a-difference blocks) and so on. The point to keep in mind is that you can develop a number of ideas to give players motivation to strive for success.

GRADING SYSTEM

A grading system that I employ to evaluate my players' and unit's performance involves assessing how well they do on each play according to the following grading categories, involving the following criteria:

- (+) = Execution: Indicates the player executed his assignment by not giving the defender an opportunity to make the play regardless of the technique employed.
- (-) = No Execution: Indicates the player attempts to execute his assignment, but regardless of his technique (correct or incorrect), he is unsuccessful in eliminating the defender from the play. The player may also have taken a play off and loafed on a snap.
- (=) = Mental Error: Indicates a mental error, where the blocker applies his blocking assignment incorrectly (goes after the wrong defender) or doesn't attempt to block anyone. For example, bust, sack, penalty.
- (S) = Big Play: Indicates outstanding play such as: the player executed his assignment and dominated his opponent, made two blocks, hustled down field to spring a running back or wide receiver for a big play or touchdown, or basically executed a great second effort.
- (WIN) = WINNER: Indicates the player executed his assignment, grading out at eighty percent or more.

A player should be given one point for every plus play, zero points for every minus, a minus two points for every double minus, and an additional two points for every big play. In calculating his overall performance, you should add up the total number of points the player earned, then divide it into the total number of plays he participated in to get his efficiency percentage. Table 10-1, 10-2, and 10-3 provide examples of individual and unit grade sheet, a composite grade sheet, and coaches game overview, repectively.

TABLE 10-1. OL GRADE SHEET.

GAME ______________ **(+) EXECUTION (-) NON EXECUTION (=) MENTAL ERROR (S) BIG PLAY**

PLAY	LT:				LG:				C:				RG:				RT:			
	BUST	SACK	PEN	LOAF	BUST	SACK	PEN	LOAF	BUST	SACK	PEN	LOAF	BUST	SACK	PEN	LOAF	BUST	SACK	PEN	LOAF
	GRADE				GRADE				GRADE				GRADE				GRADE			
PLAY	LT:				LG:				C:				RG:				RT:			
	BUST	SACK	PEN	LOAF	BUST	SACK	PEN	LOAF	BUST	SACK	PEN	LOAF	BUST	SACK	PEN	LOAF	BUST	SACK	PEN	LOAF
	GRADE				GRADE				GRADE				GRADE				GRADE			
PLAY	LT:				LG:				C:				RG:				RT:			
	BUST	SACK	PEN	LOAF	BUST	SACK	PEN	LOAF	BUST	SACK	PEN	LOAF	BUST	SACK	PEN	LOAF	BUST	SACK	PEN	LOAF
	GRADE				GRADE				GRADE				GRADE				GRADE			
PLAY	LT:				LG:				C:				RG:				RT:			
	BUST	SACK	PEN	LOAF	BUST	SACK	PEN	LOAF	BUST	SACK	PEN	LOAF	BUST	SACK	PEN	LOAF	BUST	SACK	PEN	LOAF
	GRADE				GRADE				GRADE				GRADE				GRADE			
PLAY	LT:				LG:				C:				RG:				RT:			
	BUST	SACK	PEN	LOAF	BUST	SACK	PEN	LOAF	BUST	SACK	PEN	LOAF	BUST	SACK	PEN	LOAF	BUST	SACK	PEN	LOAF
	GRADE				GRADE				GRADE				GRADE				GRADE			
PLAY	LT:				LG:				C:				RG:				RT:			
	BUST	SACK	PEN	LOAF	BUST	SACK	PEN	LOAF	BUST	SACK	PEN	LOAF	BUST	SACK	PEN	LOAF	BUST	SACK	PEN	LOAF
	GRADE				GRADE				GRADE				GRADE				GRADE			

TABLE 10-2. OL COMPOSITE GRADE SHEET.

NAME	TOTAL				RUN GAME				PASS GAME				OVERALL PERFORMANCE				
	+	-	TP	%	+	-	TP	%	+	-	TP	%	ERR	SCK	PEN	LOAF	WIN

TABLE 10-3. COACHES GAME OVERVIEW.

Date:______________________________

Opponent:__________________________

Final score:________________________

Additional factors affecting game:

____

____

Penalties:__________________________

____

Sacks:_____________________________

____

Mental errors:______________________

____

General comments (unit's performance):

General comments (specific player's performance):

Player:____________________________

____

____

Player:____________________________

____

____

Player:____________________________

____

____

Player:____________________________

____

____

Player:____________________________

____

____

Player:____________________________

____

____

CHAPTER 11

GUIDELINES FOR PERFORMING DRILLS

Drills for offensive linemen can be categorized into five basic areas:

- Agility
- Reaction
- Techniques and fundamentals
- Conditioning
- Game situations

It is important to consistently structure and evaluate your drills on the following factors — purpose, objective, coaching points, technique, and the equipment needed to execute the drills. Each drill should be designed either as a contact or non-contact activity. Which type will depend on the nature of the drill and the purpose for doing the drill. A well-designed drill can serve a player's need for both a learning experience and an opportunity to condition himself to develop excellent habits and skills on a sound basis.

Over the years, I have concluded that four keys exist for achieving maximum results when drilling a player:

- The ability to coach and teach.
- The ability to confront and demand.
- The ability to be a master of the drills you are teaching.
- The conditioning phase of coach and player.

THE ABILITY TO COACH AND TEACH

While teaching implies many things, it is simply nothing more than hard work and sound preparation. As a coach, you must know your position assignments and techniques inside and out. Your teaching package must be sound, thorough, and well organized. To attain maximum results and performance, the key ingredient is your "preparation" both on and off the field. If there is something you don't know, you should find it out, study it, and learn how to coach it. As coaches, we must constantly search for better techniques, terms and other methods to make us better. We owe it to the players and the staff. There are many coaches who violate this coaching responsibility. They assume too many things and really don't work at improving themselves as coaches. Because the game changes in cycles, we must do our part to make adjustments as needed and to continue to learn so that we can be well-prepared and organized. It really comes down to a simple axiom — "what you put into the game is what you get out of the game."

THE ABILITY TO CONFRONT AND DEMAND

Confronting your players and demanding their very best has to be done on a consistent basis. Such an approach has to be directed at everyone — from your best players, all the way down to your worst players. In the long run, this step will promote fairness, motivation, and a clear line between right and wrong. In addition, it can serve as a constant checkpoint for every player to see that they reach or go beyond their potential.

THE ABILITY TO BE A DRILL MASTER

Every coach should know his coaching package and run the drills selected with intensity and precision. Accept nothing but the best. Success at drills is nothing more than repetition, plus great effort. There is an "old adage" that goes like this, "if you give quality you'll get quality."

CONDITIONING PHASE OF COACH AND PLAYER

Both the players and coaches need to be well conditioned in order to achieve maximum results. A player must be sufficiently fit to practice hard every play, every day during practice. When a player is fatigued, he loses concentration, and his fundamentals become sloppy. Because a poorly conditioned player cannot withstand the rigors of practice and, as a result, will lose execution and performance, he greatly reduces his likelihood for improving. It is also important for the coach to be in some sort of physical shape so he can also fulfill his responsibilities with great intensity, enthusiasm, and awareness. A tired coach will often put forth an average coaching performance. Remember, your players are a direct reflection of you. It is a two-way street for both the player and coach to have the ability to practice consistently well — day after day. Nothing less is acceptable.

HOW TO RUN DRILLS

The following guidelines and suggestions can help a coach design, execute, and teach the drills he chooses to employ:

- Organize each drill according to purpose and the equipment needed to execute the drill.
- Drill for a purpose, and select drills, which meet that purpose.
- Present the drill properly (i.e., everyone must understand the drill).
- Always start the drill with a command on cadence; stop the drill with a whistle.
- Keep drills moving; repetition is the greatest teacher.
- Keep the drill simple; don't be too complicated or too involved.
- Select drills that teach reaction, resistance, and impact.
- Keep drill lines to a minimum; the best system is three players in a line.
- Fit your drills to a specific plan that achieves a learning progression.
- Always place veteran players first in line; let the young ones learn by watching.
- When bags are used, require the bag holder to hold the bag properly to create a good blocking surface.
- Inform the players on the purpose of the drill (when players know why and how to perform a drill, their performance is improved).
- Use the drill to simulate game situations.
- Demand 100% concentration and effort.
- Don't let a player go through a drill incorrectly; if he makes a mistake, stop the drill, and correct his mistakes immediately.
- Whenever possible, select competitive drills vs. defense.
- Make the drills short, crisp, and exact.
- Use a variety of drills in order to create greater interest, while accomplishing the same objective.
- Coach on the run, be enthusiastic, and build confidence.
- Don't have too many drills that overlap with other drills.
- When correcting a player's mistake, point out the reasons for your feedback (i.e., because you did this, you should do this, etc.); provide corrective criticism.
- Praise your players when they're doing a great job.
- Confront and demand – be consistent with everyone, from those players on the first team to the last walk on.
- Do not pick on a weak player to set an example.
- Coach with enthusiasm and constructive communication; demonstrate each drill.

CHAPTER 12

CONDITIONING OFFENSIVE LINEMEN

This section contains four of the basic components that linemen should work on in the off-season to prepare themselves for a productive season. Adhering to the guidelines in this section can help your players reach their potential.

FLEXIBILITY

The muscles must be able to produce and absorb power while being stretched and loaded. The lack of dynamic flexibility is a leading cause of poor athletic ability and injury. Power and flexibility often go together. Properly stretching can pay great dividends in a player's performance where it really counts — on the field.

Warming up and cooling down must be combined with, and followed by, 10 minutes of total body stretching. Flexibility is a basic component of physical fitness that can be developed with proper training. Through proper stretching, your muscles tend to become more resilient as the range of motion that they can go through increases. The net result is to improve athletic ability and decrease the risk of injury. Stretching should not be limited to the time before and after workout sessions. Players should stretch between their other conditioning exercises, spending every spare moment stretching out. If stretching is to have a beneficial effect, each rep must be held long enough to allow the reflex to subside. The suggested protocol is to stretch each muscle group for 15 to 20 seconds, relax, and repeat. You should be able to go a little further with each successive rep.

AGILITY

Agility is the ability to change directions quickly and efficiently, while maintaining balance, body control and foot speed. It is a trainable motor skill. In my opinion, good foot work is a greater asset than having blazing speed. Quickness and agility are primary elements of the total conditioning program. Having great strength is not necessarily an asset if you can't gain the initial position on your opponent on a consistent basis. You must be able to control your own body before you can control your opponent. Agility is nothing more than the ability to change directions with quickness and ease of movement in response to fast-changing situations. Agility is a function of reaction time, speed, strength, balance, body size, and technique. When performing agility drills repeatedly over time, the player's reaction time and movement ability will be improved. A retention of learning occurs, however, and results in the development and refinement of various muscular movements. This improvement enables the player to react more quickly and more decisively when confronting an opponent, thus giving the player an advantage.

In this regard, one common factor to agility is speed. By routinely performing drills that emphasize form running, mechanics of running style, quickness and flexibility, the player's potential for speed can be improved. It is very important to emphasize to your players, when they perform agility drills, that they give 100 percent. Quickness, agility and speed can't be developed by performing these drills without heart and desire.

STRENGTH

While the need for power is obvious, it is best developed by performing explosive movements. It is not developed, beyond a certain point, by doing slow heavy mass building movements. Everyone has encountered players who are strong but not very athletic, largely due to their lack of speed strength. Thus, in addition to performing heavy exercises to develop a strength base, they must perform Olympic-style weightlifting movements (hang cleans), as well as structural-type exercises (such as squats) in an explosive manner. During the off-season, I feel it is important for players to lift four days a week. They should lift two days a week during the season to maintain their strength. The off-season program consists of upper body work on Monday and Thursday and lower body work on Tuesday and Friday. Each week consists of a heavy day on Monday and Tuesday, and a light day during Thursday and Friday workouts.

METABOLIC CONDITIONING

Lifting weights alone will not get an athlete into playing shape. Lifting primarily changes the neural and structural aspects of muscles. Conditioning exercises, such as sprints, gassers, shuttles, and interval running, affect metabolic fitness to a greater extent. We have all seen players who lose it after running a few sprints because they are not conditioned. Simply put, all the strength and speed in the world will do players no good if they wear down over the course of a practice or game. More troubling is if players can't recover fully between the whistle or the drive series. They cannot be effective players if they are fatigued. Once an endurance base is established, they are ready to perform sprint intervals to enhance their speed and strength throughout the game, and improve on their recovery time in between plays and series. Remember, metabolic conditioning is sport-specific.

A sample of the metabolic drills that an offensive line can use to get into playing shape (i.e., develop their level of metabolic conditioning) involves the following:

5S = Sprint 5 yds	5BP = Backpedal 5 yds
10S = Sprint 10 yds	10SHL = Shuffle left 10 yds
10SHR = Shuffle right 10 yds	15PL = Pull left 15 yds
15PR = Pull right 15 yds	15BP = Backpedal 15 yds
20S = Sprint 20 yds	40S = Sprint 40 yds

SET 1	SET 2	SET 3	SET 4	SET 5	SET 6
5S	40S	10S	5BP	40S	15BP
15PR	10SHR	40S	15PL	10SHL	10SHL
10S	15BP	40S	20S	5BP	20S
20S	10SHL	10SHL	15PL	40S	15PR
15PL	15BP	15BP	20S	20S	40S
10SHL	15PR	15PR	10SH	15PL	5S
5BP	10SHR	10S	15BP	10S	5BP

Metabolic Drills: Offensive Line

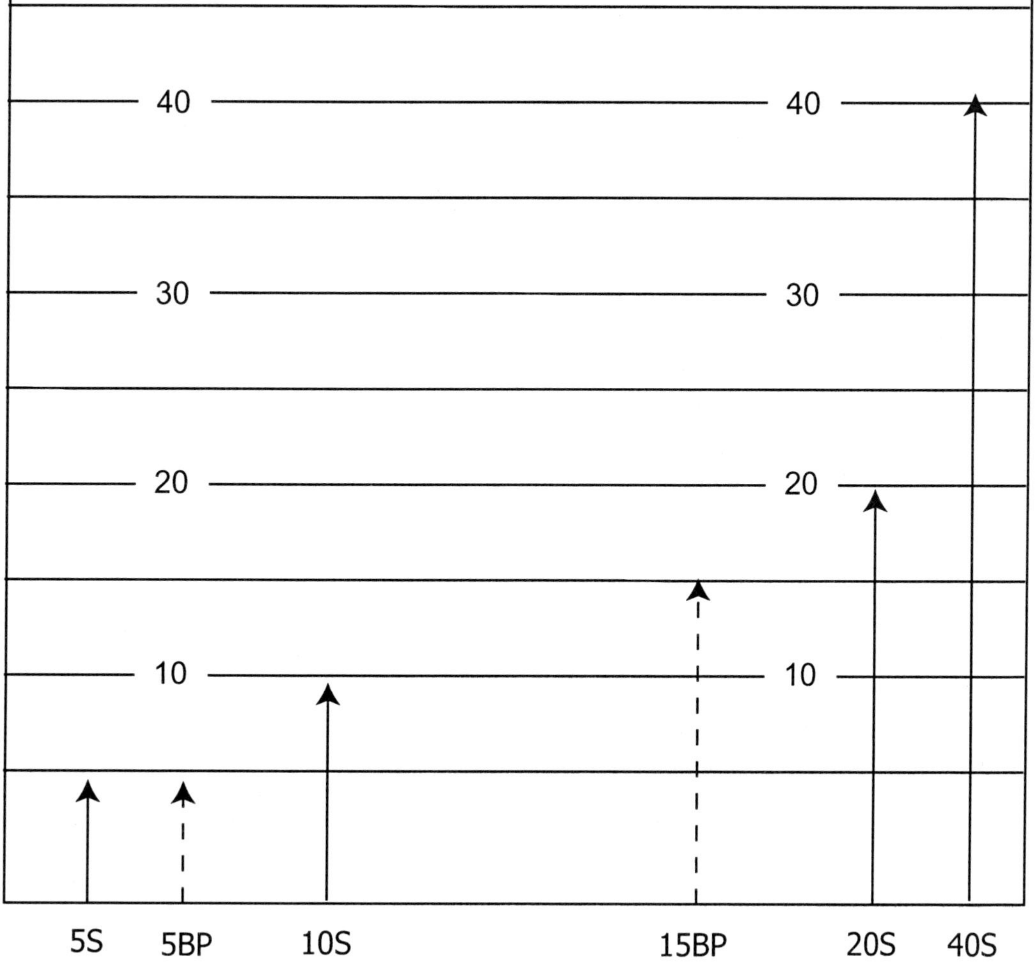

CHAPTER 13

LONG-SNAPPING TECHNIQUES

The ability to snap the ball back to the holder and punter is the number one priority of a snapper. The snap must be performed with speed, accuracy and good technique. It is important to stress the fundamentals that a snapper must diligently practice. A snapper must become confident and consistent in getting the job done by practicing and developing great technique and concentration. A player who desires to improve his snapping techniques should adhere to the coaching points, guidelines, and suggestions reviewed in this chapter.

PRACTICE ROUTINE

You should practice an average of at least 15 to 30 minutes a day, in order to master the fundamentals and skills of being a snapper. Your snapping workout can be broken down into two phases.

- Individual drills with a partner (the daily routine prior to snapping).
- Actual snapping to a holder, punter, or stationary target.

STRETCHING ROUTINE

It is important that you stretch before snapping. The key areas that you should stretch are the groin, hamstrings, arms, lower back, shoulders and wrists. Finish stretching with the clock stretch by spreading your feet as wide as possible, with your back flat and knees slightly bent, your arms extended out in front of you, and your hands together. Start the stretch at twelve o'clock going clockwise, then repeat counter clockwise. Touch both hands at each number of the clock during the rotation.

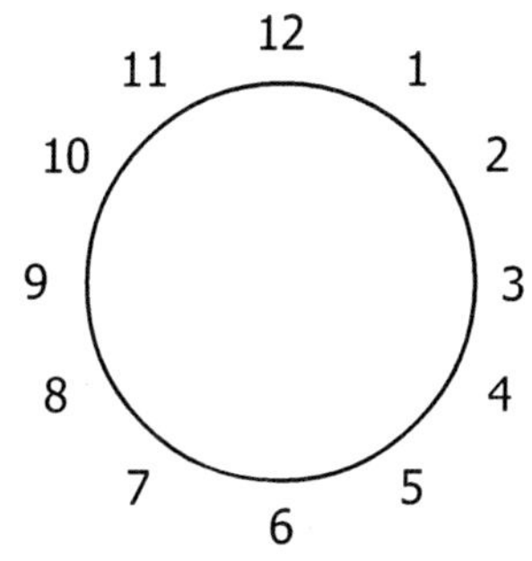

Clock stretch visual guide.

SNAPPING PROGRESSION

Stance

It is very important to feel comfortable in your stance. Point your toes straight ahead with your feet parallel and your weight equally distributed on your big toes and heels. The width of your feet should be no wider than your shoulders. It is important to have a good solid base, which allows you to lower your body to the ground. This base will create a good solid foundation from which to operate. Your back is flat, and your knees are bent, forming a Z in the knees. Bend your knees as needed for comfort. Your weight must be equally distributed between the insteps of your feet, ankles, knees and hips. Next, lay your stomach on your thighs for support. The goal is to have complete movement of your arms, through your lower body, without loosing balance and body control.

Hand Placement

Extend both arms directly in front of your shoulders and place them on the football. The bottom tip of the football should be aligned directly under your chin. Place your dominant hand, the "power hand", on the ball gripping the laces, similar to how a quarterback grips the football. The off hand is the "guide hand". It is placed on the middle of the ball, opposite of the "power hand". The middle finger should be aligned parallel to the seam of the ball, pressing the palm into the ball, forcing it into the "power hand". Now, roll and cock the "power hand", forming a slight bend in the wrist, turning the laces of the ball toward the ground.

POWER HAND PLACEMENT

- Place the first knuckle of the index finger across the seam of the ball.
- Place the middle finger and ring finger knuckles between the second and third places of the ball, keeping them close together.
- Place the little finger across the bottom seam of the ball.
- Place the thumb around the ball, forming a natural V with the index finger and thumb.

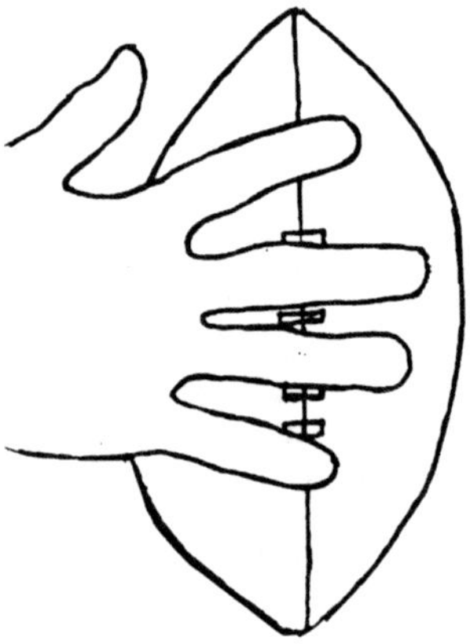

Power hand placement.

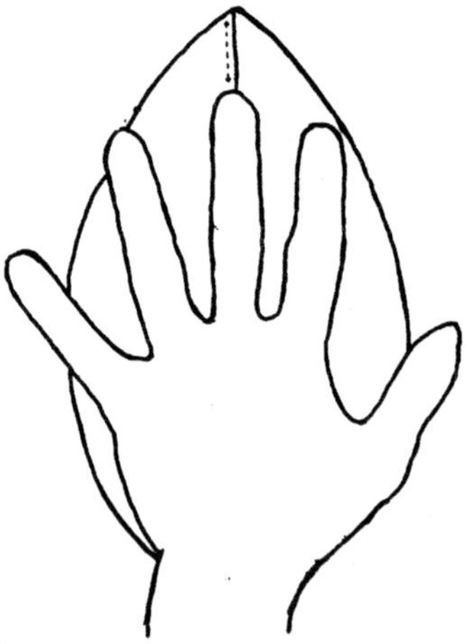

Guide hand placement.

GUIDE HAND PLACEMENT

- Place the middle finger down the seam of the ball. (The height of the middle finger on the seam helps determine elevation on the snap of the ball.)
- Place the index and ring finger on the ball, keeping them close to the middle finger.
- Line up the thumb and little finger straight across from each other for balance and a straight release.
- At the start of the snapping action, press the palm of the hand into the ball.

Such a step accomplishes three things: forces the ball into the power hand; assists the cocking action of the power hand; and puts pressure on the ball for a tight spiral.

ARM POSITION

As you grip the ball, favor your right leg with the ball if you are right-handed. If you are left-handed, favor your left leg with the ball. Then, roll and cock the ball a half turn, pointing the knuckles and laces of the power hand and ball to the ground. Keep the ball flat on the ground with the nose slightly tilted up. The guide-hand arm must be straight (i.e., elbow not bent). The arm of the power hand should be extended out in front of the body as far as possible with a slight bend in the elbow. It is important not to put a lot of weight on the football. When you are ready to deliver the snap, push the palm of the guide hand into the ball. This step will force the ball into the power hand. As a result, you're ready to fire.

SNAPPING MOTION

The snap is made with the arms, wrists and hands moving together in one continuous motion. As the snap is made, both your hands and arms follow through directly at the target. Both hands should snap through your legs as far as possible. It is important to not let your arms and hands spread after the snap. Snapping is strictly all arms and wrists. After the follow-through, snap your head up and set back off the line of scrimmage. You should be ready to protect your area and get to your coverage assignment.

INDIVIDUAL SNAPPING DRILLS

Under Hand Pass

This drill is designed to develop strength in the wrist of the power hand, and to enhance the ability to control the ball from the grip to the spiral with accuracy. Stand facing your partner at a distance of eight to 10 yards with the feet shoulder-width apart. Execute the under hand pass without taking a step toward your partner. You should concentrate on accuracy, speed, a tight spiral and follow-through. (15-20 reps)

One Hand Pass

This drill emphasizes proper positioning of the power hand, which will keep the ball from wobbling. Stand facing your partner at a distance of eight to 10 yards with the feet shoulder-width apart. Pass the ball without stepping, emphasizing accuracy, a tight spiral and speed to the target. (15-20 reps)

Two Handed Pass

In this stance, you should focus on the importance of the power hand and the guide hand working in unison toward the target. Again, the follow-through is very important. Stand facing your partner at a distance of 10 to 15 yards. It is important that the power hand is on the laces of the ball. The guide hand is spread out evenly, with the middle finger parallel on the seam of the ball. (Follow the hand placement routine.) Position the ball overhead, cock the wrist, and snap the ball to the target. Snap the wrist and point the thumbs at the target as the ball is released. The hands must work in unison, snapping the ball toward the target, emphasizing the snapping motion from the arms and wrists. Have your partner give you several locations to aim for, and change your distance. Remember, it is important to begin with the proper grip before delivering each snap. (15-20 reps)

Follow Through Snap Drill

The purpose of this drill is to emphasize the importance of the follow through and the wrist snap. The snapper should address the ball in the pre-snap position. His partner is one-yard deep behind the snapper in a quarterback position, with his palms facing downward and extended outward beneath the snapper's tail. The snapper begins the snapping motion with the hands and arms, executing proper follow through. Both the guide hand and power hand snap through the legs as far as possible, slapping the palms of your partner's hands. After maximum follow-through, the snapper should snap his head up. Do 15-20 reps in rapid succession.

Live-Snap Drill

Snap to a partner or a stationary target beginning at a depth of 10 yards, then working up to a depth of 12 to 14 yards. The snap must be done with accuracy, good technique and speed. It is important not to hitch or give away the delivery of your snap. Also, it is important to change your rhythm. It is crucial to focus on your target and to stress good technique to develop the accuracy, consistency and speed of your snap. Remember, "practice for success, part-timers equal failure."

GENERAL COACHING POINTS

- Approach the ball separately each time you snap in practice situations. Always reset your feet.
- Vary the rhythm you use in snapping the ball so that your opponents can't "zero in" on your snapping motion and rhythm.
- Throw strikes. Your landmark is inside the punter's kicking hip or kicking leg's thigh.
- Do not aim the ball. Snap it with good technique, speed, accuracy, and follow-through.
- Strive to get the ball back in 0.7 to 0.8 tenths of a second. The risk of getting a punt blocked goes up each tenth of a second beyond 0.9.
- The total elapsed time (combined snap and punt get-off time) of the snapper getting the ball back in 0.7 to 0.8 tenths of a second and the punter getting it off in 1.3 to 1.2 seconds will be 2.0 seconds.

- The long-snap routine is to get your feet set and emphasize the spring in your knees with your weight centered on the insteps. Take a look at the target before you set your hands on the ball. Approach the ball with everything in line at high noon with your body and the ball, using a correct grip, your wrist cocked and your back flat. Try to pre-cock your hips on the setup and eliminate the hitch. As you snap the ball, work back on the tracks with your feet, and follow through to your target. The long snap is all arms and hips using good concentration and focus. Pre-set your feet after each snap and repeat the routine.
- The short-snap routine is the same sequence as the long snap routine. The only exception is that your feet have very little movement on the snap. The aiming point is the back armpit of the holder, using upper body strength. Remember to vary the rhythm of your snap.

SECTION II

RUN BLOCKING

CHAPTER 14

FUNDAMENTAL PRINCIPLES OF BLOCKING

To be a fundamentally tough and sound unit, each member of the team must know what is required. Blocking can be developed to a greater degree than any other phase of football, because it is the most unnatural task. It requires patience and many hours of hard work.

The more fundamentals and techniques your players can master, the easier it will be for them to adjust to various situations. Repetition must be accepted as a way of life for an offensive lineman. Linemen must have concentration, self-discipline, an ability to communicate, and the willingness to "give it up" to their coach, knowing that he can take them farther than they can take themselves.

The following run-blocking progression sequence can be used to help a blocker to be successful:

1. Stance/alignment
   - Proper splits
   - Placement of down-hand levels
   - Balanced with flat back
   - No tipping
   - Power-producing angles
2. Start
   - Eyes on landmark (aiming point)
   - Explosive – get off on snap count
   - Short first step; maintain base
   - Maintain power-producing angles

3. Approach
    - Correct path to defender
    - Helmet priority on landmark
    - Deny penetration
4. Contact
    - Timing hand punch and hand placement
    - Hit through defender
    - Explode hips and bring feet
    - All eyes to the sky
5. Follow Through
    - Catch movement; use short driving steps
    - Chase your hands with your feet
    - Maintain body-on-body; cover your opponent up
    - Climb up and through defender's chest
    - Pound the ground and finish the block

CHAPTER 15

CAUSE OF BLOCKING FAILURES

Effective blocking by the offensive line is essential for a football team's offense to succeed. It has been estimated that 90 percent of all offensive action is blocking. Teaching proficient blocking fundamentals is an essential responsibility of the coaching staff. These techniques must be mastered and executed well if an offensive team is to be successful.

The importance of selecting a proper stance has been covered previously. The stance is based on getting a player in a good fundamental position to come off the ball, pass block, or to pull and trap on lead interference down-field. Success begins from the stance.

Getting off the ball is important, and a simple snap count aids greatly in accomplishing this objective. Two advantages the offense has over the defense is knowing both the snap count and the point of attack. Since the defense reacts to the ball, it is important that the offensive line get off on the snap count to gain an advantage and execute their assignments.

Some blocking-related problems that may need to be corrected are coming off the ball too soon, confusion in the blocking scheme, or the lack of practice with the snap count. Since the snap count starts all offensive plays, and the whistle stops and signals the end of plays, make sure to emphasize with your unit to execute each play from snap-to-whistle.

The failure of the feet to follow the hands on contact (i.e., being overextended) is a common error. Playing high, losing your base, and your center of gravity is another concern. Blocking schemes often fail when a lineman does not make contact quickly with his opponent, enabling him to finish him off. The lineman can also lose his power-producing angles by not moving his feet after contact.

Among the common causes of blocking failures are the following:

- Poor stance – failure to operate from a good base stance.
- Tipping stance by leaning, pointing, or being heavy or light handed in the pre-snap position.
- Poor alignment, splits, or hand level placement
- Slow get-off; unsure of the snap count.
- Poor first step – lunging, overextended, or losing base and body control.
- Ignorance of assignment; poor concentration.
- No punch; poor contact; no blow delivery.
- Poor landmark on defender prior to contact.
- Losing base, power-producing angles, and control of the defender.
- Failure to use proper technique to carry out assignment.
- Loafing – lack of aggressiveness or hustle.

CHAPTER 16

GENERAL OFFENSIVE LINE FOOTBALL TERMS

PLAYSIDE:	The callside of the formation to the point of attack.
BACKSIDE:	The callside of the formation away from the point of attack.
L.O.S.:	Abbreviation for line of scrimmage.
P.O.A.:	The area/landmark where the football is to cross the LOS.
CALLS:	A verbal signal given by a lineman to indicate particular blocking scheme. Usually delivered at the LOS by playside and backside lineman.
GAP:	The area between the shoulder or foot of one offensive lineman and the shoulder or foot of the adjacent offensive lineman; also can also be used as a call on blocking scheme or protection.
SPLITS:	The size of the gaps between offensive lineman; these areas may vary according to the play called.
LEVELS:	A landmark point where offensive lineman will place their hands as they set into 3-point stance. This point will vary according to the play called.

BOX:	The area between the LOS to the defensive linebacker depth– from tackle-to-tackle or tackle-to-tight end.
FRONT:	A verbal call given by the center to indicate the number of down linemen and the number of linebackers in the box.
P.S.L.B.:	The inside or outside linebacker aligned to the playside of the center.
B.S.L.B:	The inside linebacker aligned backside or over the center.
EMLOS:	End man on the line of scrimmage.
OVERHANG:	Walked-up defender on LOS outside the defensive end.
SUGAR:	Inside linebacker walked up into the LOS between the tackles.
COMBOS:	A verbal signal given by a lineman to indicate a particular blocking combination. Usually delivered at the LOS by the center, and the covered or uncovered lineman playside and backside of the play.
LEVEL ONE:	Area that identifies the down lineman across the LOS on the defensive side of the ball.
LEVEL TWO:	Area beyond level one that identifies linebackers on the defensive side of the ball.
LEVEL THREE:	Area beyond level two that identifies the secondary players on the defensive side of the ball.

CHAPTER 17

THE TEN COMMANDMENTS OF RUN BLOCKING

The 10 commandments of run blocking should be addressed and demanded, on a consistent basis, with your players. Include every player from the best to the worst. This approach promotes fairness, truth, and the difference between right and wrong. These commandments can be used as a motivational factor and a constant checklist for every player to master their techniques in the run game.

1. ASSIGNMENT

2. STANCE

3. ALIGNMENT

4. SPLITS

5. LANDMARK

6. GET OFF

7. APPROACH

8. CONTACT

9. LEVERAGE

10. FOLLOW THROUGH

CHAPTER 18

DEFENSIVE FRONT RECOGNITION

Note: the center is responsible for making defensive-front calls.

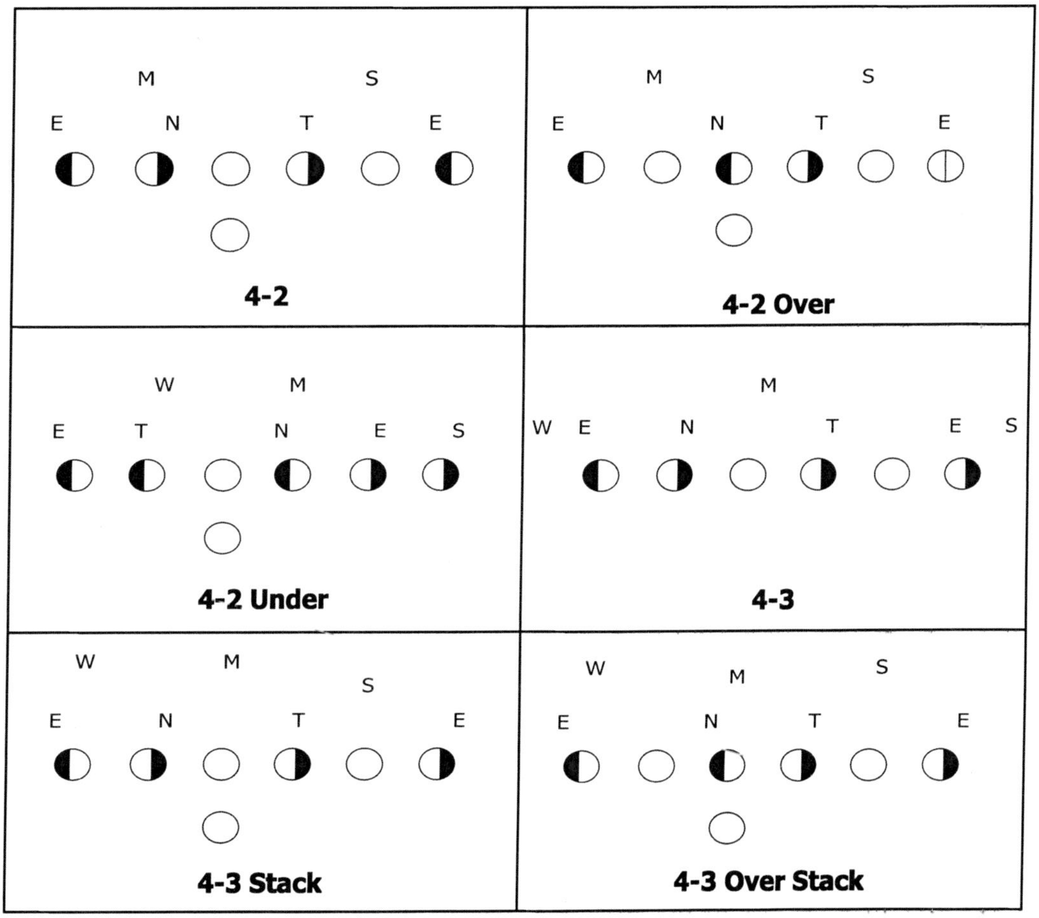

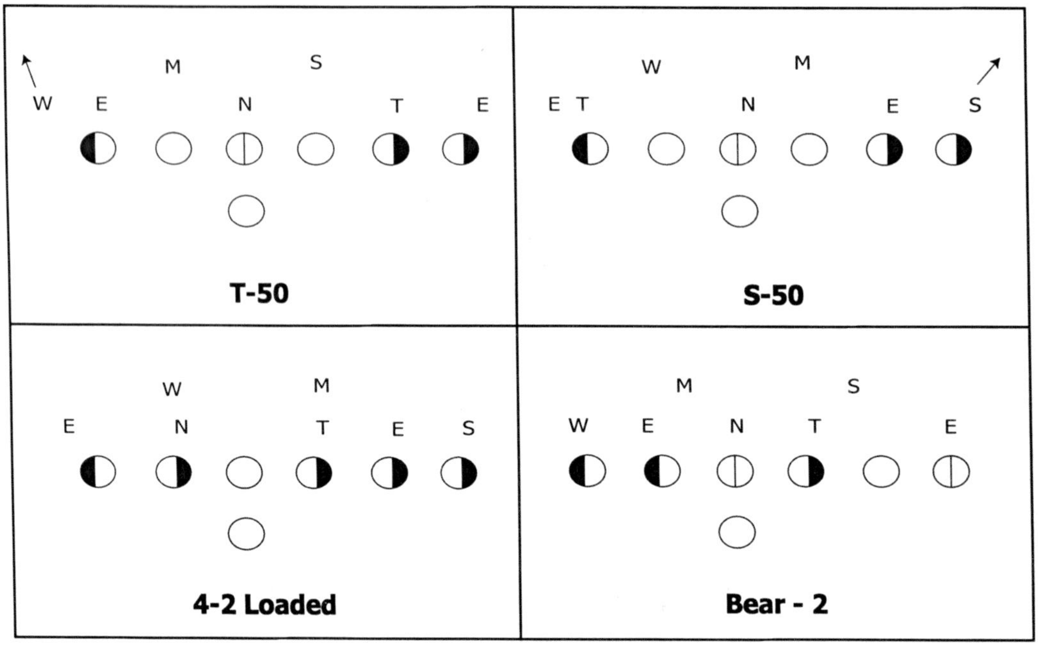
M
S
W
E
N
T
E
T-50
W
M
E T
N
E
S
S-50
W
M
E
N
T
E
S
4-2 Loaded
M
S
W
E
N
T
E
Bear - 2

CHAPTER 19

DEFENSIVE NUMBERING SYSTEM

Numbers are assigned to defensive linemen according to how they line up against the offensive linemen. This system allows a team to communicate a defender's alignment and technique, as well as the gap for which they are responsible.

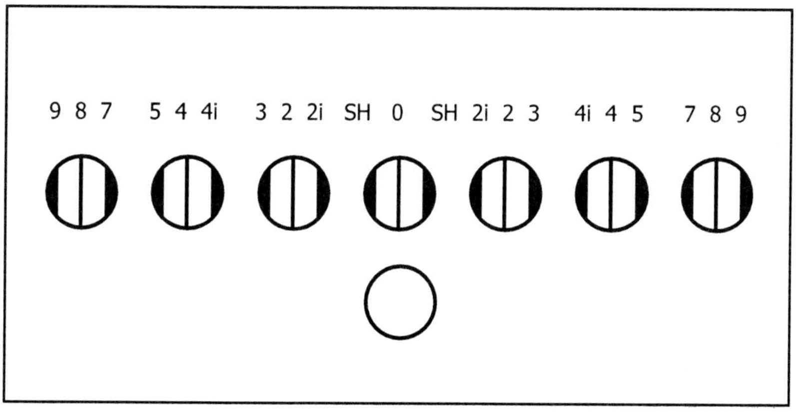

GAP IDENTIFICATION

Gaps between lineman are identified using the following letters as shown:

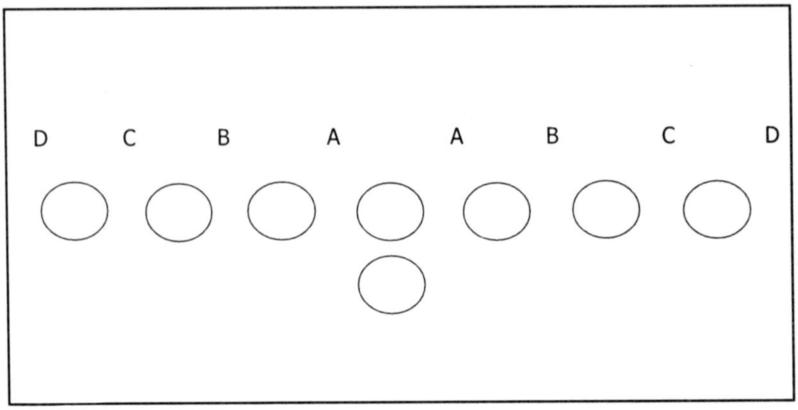

"A" gap = Between the center and guard

"B" gap = Between the guard and tackle

"C" gap = Between the tackle and tight end

"D" gap = Outside the tight end

HOLE NUMBERING SYSTEM

The running attack points are based on a number in the space between the offensive lineman. Holes to the right of the center are even numbers (0, 2, 4, 6, 8), while holes to the left of the center are odd numbers (1, 3, 5, 7, 9).

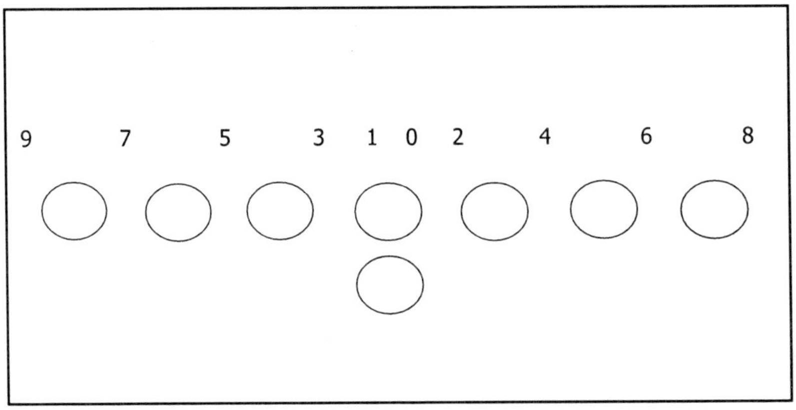

CHAPTER 20

COMMUNICATION

Teams must be able to communicate on the line of scrimmage (LOS). This is an area of development on which we focus. We stress the following points to our players:

CLARIFICATION OF ALIGNMENT Conceivably, an alignment could be called on every snap. Accordingly, a call must be made to clear up any confusion. When in doubt, call a defender's alignment. The following diagrams illustrate examples of various defensive alignments.

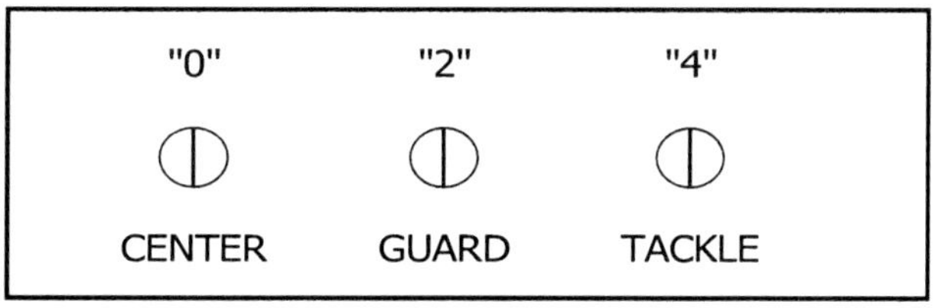

Head-up alignment.

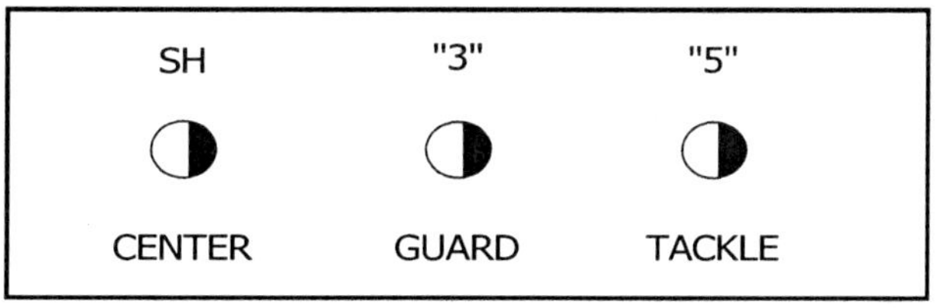

Outside-shade alignment.

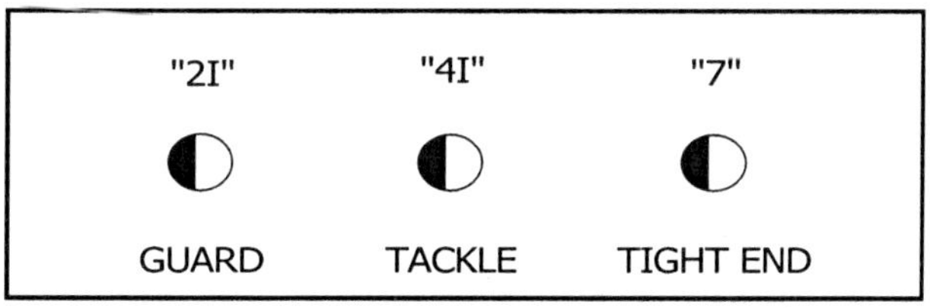

Inside-shade alignment.

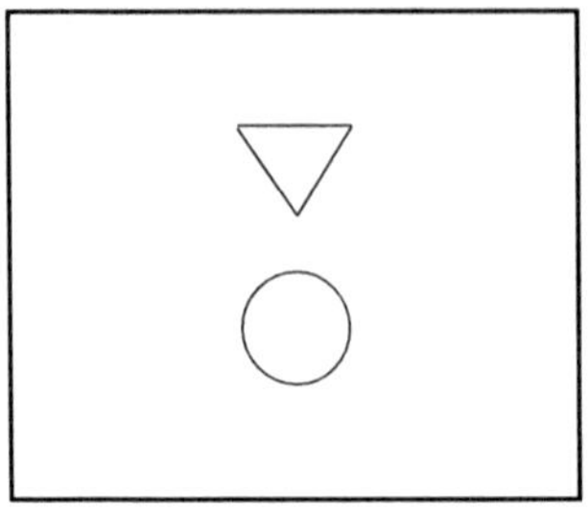

Covered alignment.

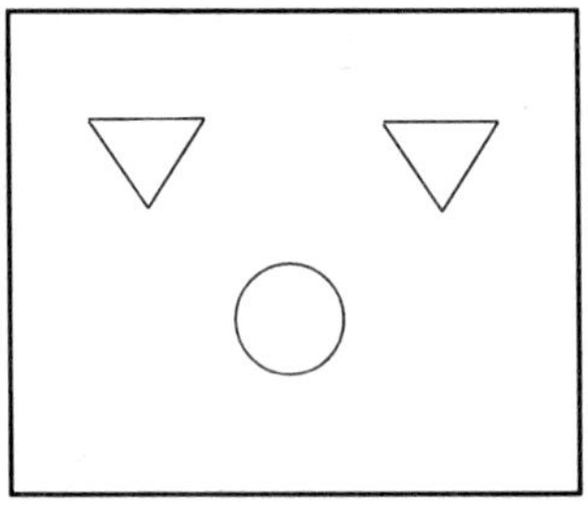

Uncovered alignment.

CONFIRMING BLOCKING SCHEMES. Any multiple scheme can be clarified by reinforcing the scheme to be used. The covered lineman should make the call. Several examples of such calls include the following:

- "ACE"
- "DUECE"
- "SWIPE"
- "SLIP"

CALL ADJUSTMENTS. From time to time, a scheme must be changed or adjusted to get better angles.

CONFIRMING DEFENSIVE ALIGNMENTS. A team must be able to clarify the defensive alignment. While the quarterback will check plays at the LOS, the offensive linemen must identify certain schemes for themselves. This capability is essential versus stacked defenses.

AN EXAMPLE OF COMMUNICATION

The alignment of defenders on the LOS at the point of attack must be identified.

PST is the apex blocker. PST starts the call, which is then passed down the line.

Calls:

FST = "Trey"

FSG = "Ace"

C = "Ace"

BSG = "Man"

BST = "Sift"

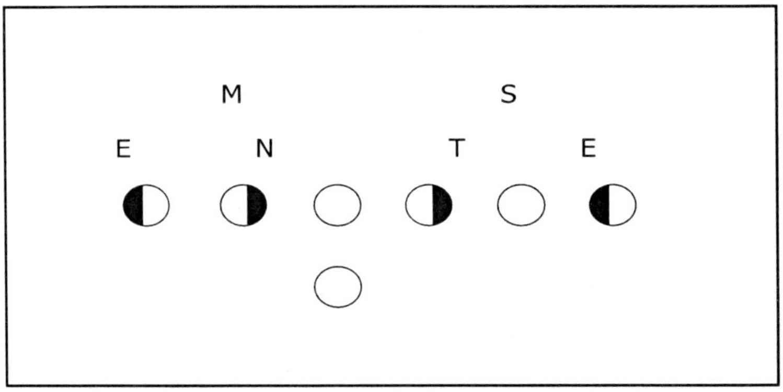

32 Scat vs. a 4-2 defense.

DISTINGUISHING BETWEEN FRONTS. The center can clear things up a great deal if he can identify defensive alignments. This information must be communicated by the center by making a front call. The two following examples illustrate this responsibility.

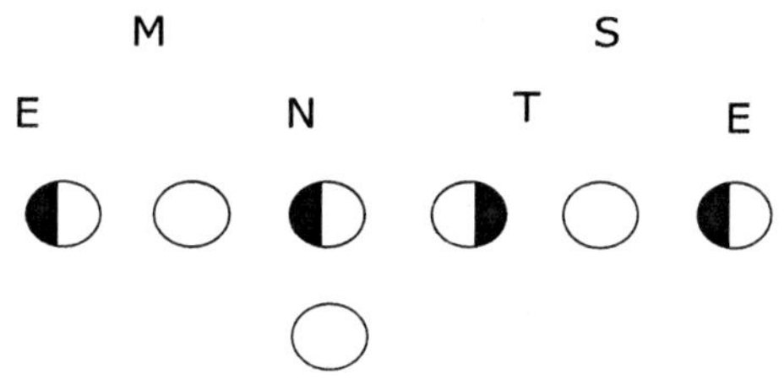

4-2 OVER RT

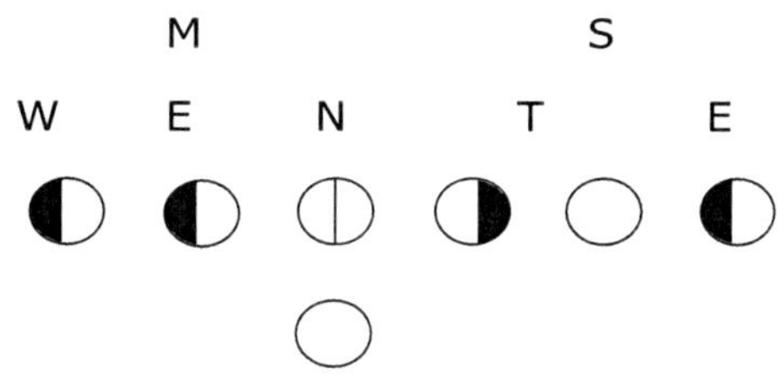

BEAR 2

USING AUXILIARY CALLS. Auxiliary calls are used to gain an advantage in blocking schemes. An example of an auxiliary call is "BOLT". The guard makes this call. Against a 2i defender on the backside guard, it is very tough for the backside guard to cutoff or to maintain an inside position. The "BOLT" call gives the offensive linemen a better blocking angle. The center and backside guard change blocking assignments. (The auxiliary calls are matched up with proper plays only.)

CHAPTER 21

BASIC FUNDAMENTALS OF OFFENSIVE LINE PLAY

HUDDLE

Forming the huddle is the responsibility of the offensive center. In this regard, he must be coached and encouraged to take pride in doing his job well. The huddle is where it all begins; the players must be able to listen and hear. If effective communication is not established in the huddle, the chances of getting off a productive play are slim-to-none. The lack of huddle discipline, a situation in which players other than the quarterback talk, leads to confusion, and miscommunication. As the quarterback steps into the huddle, all eyes should be directly on him. Good focus and concentration will prevent mistakes in formation alignment, getting off the ball late on the snap count, running the wrong way on protection schemes, or going in the wrong direction. Each player in the huddle should visualize his assignment and keep the snap count in mind. Good communication is a key ingredient for what a player is expected to do — execute properly.

SNAP COUNT

A snap count must be simple and must meet the needs of the coach's offensive philosophy. As a coach, you might consider the advantages and disadvantages of both the rhythmic and non-rhythmic cadences. Proponents of the rhythmic cadence maintain that their players get off better as an offensive unit. Regardless of the pros and cons of each type of cadence, the one selected must be developed and practiced under all conditions in order to be perfected. The choice is yours, but be consistent with your choice.

STANCE

A good stance is the key for an offensive linemen. It is his basic foundation from which he can get the job done. Everything a lineman does starts from his stance. Usually a sloppy stance occurs because of a lack of discipline or fatigue. On the other hand, it may be from a lack of coaching or over coaching. If the player has been taught a basic stance, and he is inconsistent in getting into it, the coach should check the player's body build and what he is asking him to do. Some linemen's build just does not fit into the standard stances we try to put them into. As such, their stance should be adjusted, allowing them to get into a comfortable and natural stance from which they can execute properly. Fatigue can also contribute to a player's inability to execute the correct stance. In this instance, you might consider whether your players have been conditioned well enough. Whatever the problem may be, however, you must find it, correct it, and coach it with discipline and consistency. Keep in mind that everything the players do starts from the stance. From whatever stance you choose as their base stance, your players must have the ability to transfer their weight to go in the right direction. We feature two stances in our offense; both are functional, balanced stances that will allow each blocker to maneuver in all directions.

THREE-POINT STANCE (DOWN POSITION)

The Staggered Base. The lineman's feet are spread out slightly wider than shoulder width, his feet are slightly staggered with the toe-instep relationship between up foot and back foot never greater than the toe-to-heel. A right-handed stance will require a toe-to-instep stagger, with the toes slightly turned out and pointing downfield. The weight of the body should be placed on the insteps of the feet with the entire foot on the ground with slight daylight in the back foot. The foot and toes should be open in order to allow movement in the proper direction. With knees slightly in and toes out, this positioning allows the offensive lineman to lower his center of gravity. With this stance, the power angles are enhanced, enabling a player to operate with a good, wide solid base and to maintain body control. It should be noted that a player may tilt or turn his outside leg to block the defender on an angle. He must shift his weight in his butt and hips to his inside leg or outside leg for better weight distribution. Power is then locked into his hips by rolling his knees slightly inward. The blocker now has the power-producing angles in his foot, knees, and hips. The term that can be used to describe this angle to your players is — "get a "Z" in the knees."

Down Hand. Form a five-point tripod with all of your fingers, extend and reach out with your hand. Don't allow a dead run on a pass key. Place your down hand slightly inside of the corresponding knee of the back foot, down from the shoulder with a slight flexion in the elbow. (To find the correct location of the down hand, an offensive lineman must be able to lift his hand off the ground, cup his hand, and catch his eyeball. If there is no weight shift when this occurs, then he has established a good solid base stance with proper weight distribution down the midline of his body.)

Off Hand. Place the off hand on the side of the knee with the hand cupped and relaxed, froming a slight fist on the side of the knee ready for shooting action.

Shoulders. Square the shoulders to the L.O.S. with the back flat and parallel to the ground. Keep your tail even or slightly elevated above the shoulders to put the levers of the legs in a cocked position, thereby producing power angles.

Head-Neck. Have a natural extension of the back; the head is pulled back slightly cocked, not strained.

Eyes. At the L.O.S., make a pre-snap read from left to right. The eyes scan and rotate 180 degrees, looking through the eyebrows, focusing on the target/aiming point. Proper vision cannot be emphasized enough. It is the key to recognition, anticipation and adjustment.

Note: In goal-line and short-yardage run situations, flex more at the elbows and knees to attain better explosion and pad level on the defender.

TWO-POINT STANCE (UP POSITION)

- Utilize the same base with the lower body.
- Place the thumbs on your knees on the inside of the groin.
- Keep the back ramrod straight (selling pass) with the head and eyes rotating and scanning.
- Be prepared to run block from a two-point stance. This situation is where a first sound play has an advantage.
- Keep in mind that vertical and horizontal splits are again an advantage.

COACHING POINTS FOR THE STANCE

- *Foot Pressure.* Place all the weight in the stance on the insteps in order to take power steps. Blocking adjustments are made more easily on the insteps.
- *Knock-Kneed.* Knock-kneed posture ensures that the power is locked in the hips and legs. Maximize power by maintaining a balanced center of gravity. The knocked knee also must emphasize the bent-knee demeanor.
- *Mental Weight:* Place all the weight of the lower body on the leg and foot opposite the player's first step and ensure the proper angle of departure.
- *Eyes.* Do not allow the eyes to lag behind any step-off. Focus the eyes and bring the feet to the target.

SUMMARY

The aforementioned elements can be altered slightly to fit individual physical differences, but basic points will all be the same. Many linemen are careless about their stance and quickly develop bad habits. The "little things" involving a good stance should be emphasized by correcting every mistake, no matter how minor.

COMMON FAULTS OF A BAD STANCE

- Toes ducked out too far, not pointed straight ahead.
- Weight back on heels, instead of on the balls of feet.
- Not balanced — too much weight forward or back. Tendency to telegraph run or pass.
- Too much stagger between up foot and back foot.
- Head down, not straight ahead, with eyes on the target.
- Knee not in line with ankles and feet.
- Tail too high or low, forming poor power-producing angles.
- Shoulder tipped and not square to L.O.S. The back not flat or parallel to the ground.

STARTING FROM THE STANCE

Commonly known as a "get-off" or "coming off the ball," starting from the stance should adhere to the following basic principle: anytime the lineman is covered or over any part of the blocker's body, the offensive lineman should lead and fire out with his back foot. If he is not covered, then the player should lead out with the foot nearest the defender he will block.

MECHANICS OF LINE STARTS

- Acceleration foot. The initial step must be quick, with the proper angle of departure. (The first step is not an overextended step.)
- Drive foot initiates the acceleration foot by gripping the turf with the ball of the foot and driving hard off the ground to initiate the acceleration foot.
- Roll over the front step. The first step must be over-extended. The knee must roll over in front of the toe to maintain power-producing angles and create a low blocking base to gain leverage.
- The knee of the trail leg should dip and aim towards the ground. This action will help maintain the center of gravity and the blocking base to gain leverage.
- The initial movement is forward and out, not up.
- Level off. The aiming point and landmark on the down defender are through the chin of the defender. The landmark will vary, depending on scheme of play, either between the middle line or two inches past midline on the outside number of the defender.
- The blocker's pads must be lower than the defender's in order to get and maintain leverage of the defender.

- Focus on driving the eyes at the chin on the down lineman and the bottom of the numbers on linebackers.
- Cock the hands on the first step, shooting them out as contact is made.
- The first and second steps are the most important. After the first-step gain, get the second step in the ground quickly. Do not leave the tail leg dragging; be explosive with it (catch your hands with your feet).
- Advantages of the "get off":
  - √ Cadence. Blocker knows the snap count. Defender must react to blocker's movement of the ball. Therefore, the offensive lineman has the advantage of triggering the first movement across the L.O.S.
  - √ Direction. Blocker knows where the point of attack is and the play's direction. Defender must react on snap of the ball. This factor provides angle-of-departure advantages.

CHAPTER 22

CENTER STANCE AND EXCHANGE

The stance that we use for our offensive center is a three-point stance with the weight evenly distributed on both feet and the down hand on the football. This stance provides the best opportunity to run and pass protect in our offensive system. The following "components" are stressed when teaching and coaching the center's stance and snapping technique:

- *Base feet.* The feet are shoulder width or slightly wider with toes out, pointing down the field. The feet are parallel or slightly staggered with a toe-to-instep relationship. The heels are slightly off the ground with the weight on the insteps, forming power angles at the ankles, knees, and hips. All blocking adjustments are made on the insteps of the feet for the center.
- *Shoulder-back-tail.* The shoulders are square to the L.O.S., with the back parallel (flat back) to the ground. The tail is slightly higher than the shoulders to facilitate the snap.
- *Head-neck-eyes.* The head is raised slightly and the neck is relaxed with the eyes able to see both feet.
- *Relationship of ball to center's head.* The ball is placed slightly to the right (eye to the ball) if right-handed, opposite if left-handed. The grip hand and arm are extended out as far as possible, maintaining balance. (Do not put a lot of weight on the ball.) Remember, the ball must be ahead of the center, not under him, causing a reach-out effect in the arms and shoulders.
- *Initial movement.* Step with the near foot when exploding out to block. At times, it will be necessary to shift the weight from one foot to the other before jabbing out. Remember, the snap and hit-out are one motion.

- *The Grip.* The football will be placed so that laces are either facing straight up or quarter turned to the opposite foot (this depends on how the quarterback is to receive the ball). If the laces are up, the center should grip the ball with the thumb of the grip hand between the second and third lace. If the ball is quarter turned, the grip should face a natural "V" formed between the thumb and the index finger. The fingers should grip the ball on the side to have complete control of the ball.
- *Off Hand.* The center should place his off hand on the side of the knee with his hand cupped and relaxed, forming a slight fist on the side of the knee, and have it ready for shooting action.
- *Snap Method.* When the center snaps the ball, he pumps the ball in a straight line, sliding the ball off the left cheek of his buttocks in an attempt to break the heels of the quarterback's hands apart (wedge the ball between the heel of his hands). He should bring the ball up with a stiff wrist and a lifting, pumping action, placing the ball directly in the quarterback's hand. The ball should turn a quarter naturally, a position that assures the quarterback of getting the laces and a proper grip on the ball for handing off or delivering a pass. The center should master stepping with the proper foot as he executes this pumping snap technique. The snap and step is a one motion, simultaneous movement. Remember, it is important to hear the ball "pop" as it hits the quarterback's top hand. In other words, "snap pop," and the ball fills the quarterback's hands.

SHOT-GUN SNAP

The center should assume the same stance and technique as if the quarterback was under center. His head should remain up while making this blind snap. The quarterback will be at a depth of five yards. The center's aiming point should be the quarterback's belt-line or bottom numbers. The center must flick the ball back with his wrist on a straight line. The snap line should not be changed because of the fact that it's a shot-gun snap.

CENTER/QUARTERBACK EXCHANGE MISCUES

The center/quarterback exchange is the focal point of the offensive play. Without a clean exchange, no chance exists for a successful play. Therefore, it is essential that all miscues involving the center/quarterback exchange are eliminated. The exchange must become automatic and rhythmic between the two individuals. In order for this to happen, the exchange must be practiced daily. A checklist for analyzing possible exchange problems would include the following factors for the center:

- Lifting or swinging. The ball does not break the heels, a situation which would force the quarterback to grab for the ball, coming up short.
- Ball down the middle of the crotch, causing the quarterback to get the ball at the top end of the ball.

- The center lifting his tail on the snap, rather than firing out with a flat back.
- The center placing too much weight on the ball.
- Not delivering the football hard and fast into the quarterback's hands.
- Anticipating the count or snapping the ball before the actual count. This allows the defense to react sooner and defeat the offense, and miscues the get-offs of the other offensive linemen.
- Snapping late and behind the actual count, which disrupts the quarterback's mechanics and the timing of the play.
- Overstriding on the first step, causing the ball to spray away from the quarterback's hands.
- Failure by the coach to work the centers in pre-practice with a defender on the center's nose or in the gaps.
- Not practicing center/quarterback exchanges with wet balls.
- In my experience, most fumbled snaps occur when the center is reach blocking away from the snap hand.

When miscues occur, the coach should check the center first. Quite often, the center is carrying the football with him on his first step. To reduce errors, have the center and quarterback exchange several snaps each day at practice and prior to games. As each center and quarterback are different in their technique, it is a good idea to rotate them in practice situations so that each center gets a feel for all of the quarterbacks.

CHAPTER 23

SPLITS, LEVELS, AND PRE-SHIFT

An offensive lineman is required to be knowledgeable about and have a thorough understanding of the concepts behind proper levels and splits. An offensive lineman's application of these concepts will give an offense a distinct advantage on both run and pass plays. The different splits and levels will influence what plays are being run. A list of the various types of splits and levels that can be used includes the following:

HORIZONTAL ALIGNMENT/SPLITS

- Mini: guards, tackles, and tight ends 18 inches.
- Normal: guards two feet; tackles two feet; and tight ends 2.5 feet.
- Max: guards 2.5 feet; tackles three feet; tight ends 3.5 feet.
- Tight: guards, tackles, and tight ends one foot.

To help in determining what splits to use, coaches may employ what I call "smart splits" which can vary according to the following factors:

- Defense and defensive personnel (for example, is the defense a gap defense?; is it a slant defense?).
- Offensive play and individual assignments (for example, basically plays outside tighten the splits, while plays inside widen the splits).
- The player's ability and quickness. Be realistic about what can be accomplished versus the defender and the defensive scheme.
- Goal-line and short-yardage situations.

- Passing situations (for example, drop-back, roll-out, play-action, boots, naked).

VERTICAL ALIGNMENTS/LEVELS

- Up position. The offensive lineman's toes should be parallel with the heels of the center, approximately one-yard off the ball.
- One (tight). The offensive lineman's alignment is with the down hand on the back tip of the ball, with the helmet aligned on top of center's numbers.
- Two (normal). The alignment is with the down hand on the toes of the center.
- Three (loose). The alignment is with the down hand on the arch of the center with the helmet aligned on center's jersey number.
- Four (deep). An adjustment is made with the down hand on the heels of the center with the helmet aligned on center's waistline.
- Five (stagger). An adjustment is made involving two adjacent linemen, with one being normal or loose and the other being loose or deep.

(Note: tight ends sometimes need to align on the back tip of the football in order to be affective on pass releases.)

The key to good alignment is to have the tackles aligned on the guards, and the tight ends aligned on the tackles so there is no bowing effect and no stagger. (Because of alignment responsibility and specific plays, however, one side of the line may be split and slightly deeper than the other side). The players should line up on the ball and look in at the ball to insure an outside alignment. In addition, the depth a lineman's alignment may vary with the situation. In a goal-line situation, the offensive lineman should take more of the ball. In a definite passing down, he gets off the ball more. Remember that whatever position is used, the coach should never accept a bowed line or improper splits. Because the rules specify that no lineman's head can be deeper than the center's waistline, the offensive lineman should not forget to look inside.

THE PRE-SHIFT

Some offensive teams shift from a two-point to a three-point stance. This shift will be performed according to cadence rules and the situations that make it necessary. The pre-shift is an invaluable tool of the trade. Among the advantages of a pre-shift are to help address the following factors:

- Split adjustment
- Alignment and adjustment
- Communication and anticipation

- Shifting on the down to allow a better angle to cover or reach
- The prevention of stance keys by the defense

A pre-shift provides a distinct advantage for the blocker since it puts him in the optimum position to execute his block.

The center will be responsible for an up-or-down call which locks the lineman into a two-point or three-point stance. These calls are game-planned according to situation. The pre-shift also enables the blockers to address the following situations:

- The expansion of a 3-or 5-technique.
- The constriction of splits to allow for double-team movement. Expand and constrict well.
- The elimination of a gap defender. With a man in the gap, no gap exists.
- The adjustment of the uncovered lineman back to an off alignment to view the double-team area better.

CHAPTER 24

ZONE-BLOCKING TECHNIQUES

FOOTWORK GUIDELINES AND SUGGESTIONS FOR THE INSIDE ZONE BLOCK

- Keep a "wide base" at all times, especially on contact.
- Push off the instep to allow your balance to come from the instep and create good power angles. Push off the instep flatfooted and step with the whole instep in a flatfooted manner.
- The "drop-step" is designed for a blocker to lose ground, to gain a blocking angle, and to be in a good position on a defender. Pick it up, and put it down; keep it outside the hip. Depth and width of the step are based on the alignment of the defender.
- The "drop-step" enables the blocker to create the best movement on the best angle. Do not shrink the hole, because the blocker will not be in the hole. The blocker cannot get flattened out or torqued.
- The "angle lead step" allows the blocker to "cover up" a defender on the given angle.
- The "drop-step" creates a slight shoulder turn or shoulder tilt that puts the blocker on the proper angle to cover up the defender. Shoulders tilt and hips open according to how the defender is aligned. Shoulder turn and tilt relate to the defender's alignment. The "drop-step" allows the blocker's second step to get through.
- The "slide-step" must get on the ground. The blocker should see how fast he can get his whole foot down.
- The "slide-step" allows the blocker to lower his center of gravity and buys him time to sight the target.
- The "slide-step" allows the blocker to stay gathered by keeping his shoulders between his ankles for balance and demeanor.
- The "slide-step" allows a blocker to gain a wider base so that when he strikes, he strikes with a solid base.

- The "slide-step" gives a blocker better leverage by lowering his center of gravity and enables him to strike in a stronger posture.
- The "slide-step" gives the blocker the ability to gather himself and redirect to any inside movement. This position allows him to maintain his base on blocking adjustments.
- The "drop-step and slide-step" will time up with the alignment, course, and chase lane of the running backs. The running backs should complement the line with the same turn and tilt. The running back will cause the defense to be influenced by the running back's action.
- A very important coaching point: the blocker's shoulders should surge toward the defender; they do not rise up. The blocker's upper body should go forward.

COVERED BLOCKER AT THE POINT OF ATTACK

- Assignment: reach block; technique: angle lead or reach step, punch, and finish.
- Target: two inches outside of the midline and get pad under pad.
- Lead or reach step and tilt shoulders on an angle to cover up the defender. Force the defender to make a decision. Stretch, displace, and distort the defender.
- Lead with the helmet, pads, and fist. Let the upper body go forward and surge on the angle. Punch, lift, and strain.
- Cock the arms and shift them for momentum. Thrust with the hands and then grab. Get the hands inside with upper body violence and explosion.
- Get the second step down right away slightly inside the defenders. Knee the defender in the crotch on the crossover and get movement on the angle.
- On stalemates, widen the feet quickly, activate the feet, and finish the defender when he moves to pursue.
- If the defender slants, stop and drop inside foot to come back and get a piece of him.
- If the defender widens or the blocker feels him beyond his center of gravity, then twist him out with inside arm and head – stay on his body and finish. Anticipate redirection inside.
- Ninety percent of the block is finish.
- Versus a 3-technique: the playside guard — angle lead step or drop step and punch (according to alignment).
- Versus a 5-Technique: the playside guard — drop and step and climb; playside tackle — angle lead step and double punch. (Get movement!)
- Assess depth, width, and technique of defender to establish the split, alignment, and type of step.

UNCOVERED BLOCKER AT THE POINT OF ATTACK

- The drop step should be based on the depth of the linebacker. If the linebacker is aligned deep (3-5 yards), take a deeper drop step for depth and width to buy time. If linebacker is aligned less than three yards, lead and waddle.
- Versus a slow-flow linebacker, key the linebacker. No call requires a bucket step and a one-hand technique against a slow flow linebacker. Punch and grab the playside target or utilize a flipper technique. Block the linebacker on or near the LOS.
- Versus a fast-flow linebacker or call, convert the hands to a two-hand punch and peak on the LOS. This is a two-handed double team. Get movement and push with the outside blocker. Punch extension is crucial.
- The running back must set-up the block. Timing is crucial to the blocking. The running back will bring the linebacker to the blocker. Allow the linebacker to press the LOS. It helps to understand linebacker play: fill, flow, tuff, stem, etc.
- Maintain the proper shoulder angle/shoulder tilt. Do not get squared up. Be alert to keep the playside arm "out." Stair step the alignment. Get off the ball.
- Stay in the proper "demeanor" and maintain body control. Understand that the best holes and creases are to the bubble.

CENTER AND BACKSIDE GUARD COMBO

1. Center:
    - Against a 0-technique, normal zone rules apply, drop step, and two-hand it.
    - Against a 0-technique, slant backside, stop, redirect, and put body on defender. Maintain shoulder angle and key the backside linebacker with his eyes. Hand conversion to punch.
    - Treat any backside shade as uncovered. Drop-step and work swipe progression LOS-to-second level. Work eyes and have a feel for second-level timing.
    - On a swipe progression, the backside guard will punch nose into his gap. Be alert to grab it, especially on a slant move.
    - No swipe progression on "sugar" call. Get his eyes on the backside linebacker immediately. Get movement on the double-team combination.
2. Guard:
    - Against a 0-technique and uncovered, drop-step, punch, and climb. Slant away will force you to convert and waddle to second level.
    - Against a 0-shade backside, drop-step and two-hand it on the playside target. Punch and climb. Punch the nose back on the center and get

movement. Climb for the backside run-through. If the linebacker flows fast, finish the nose hard and keep fighting with the head inside.

- "Zebra" call vs. a sugar linebacker hole.

BACKSIDE GUARD AND BACKSIDE TACKLE COMBO

1. Slip call vs. 2-technique or a 3-technique.
2. Assess the alignment of the backside linebacker. Know his alignment and execute the proper slip.
3. The backside guard and backside tackle must develop a feel and sense of timing on this play.
4. Guard:
    - Against a 2-technique, slide step and two-hand it. If he is ahead of the two, catch up by stopping or waddling. If he is behind, fight to get your head on the inside target – (still must cover up.)
    - Against a 3-technique, treat the 3-technique like you are uncovered. Upfield step and angle lead step on a 45-degree track. Utilize punch or forearm technique when blocking half a man. Read the linebacker and feel the defensive lineman. Hand convert vs. a 3-slant. Never, ever crossover.
    - Second-level adjustment based on flow of the mike or will linebacker. Ensure movement on the double team and keep the playside arm free. Alignment will force a quicker come off, but you still must work it. Mike alignment will buy you more time for more movement.
    - Be alert to a "Zebra" call vs. a sugar linebacker and stems.
    - Against a 1-technique, slide call to playside tackle. Lead step, two-hand it, and cover man up, and down the track.
5. Tackle:
    - Split and alignment key — normal split and loose alignment.
    - Drop-step and get inside vs. 3-technique. Two-hand it, and fight for movement.
    - On a "slide" call vs. a 1-technique, drop-step, punch, and climb. One-hand it while maintaining the angle of play. Get second level linebacker covered up.
    - On a "slip" call, drop-step, punch, and takeover. Against any fast flow-linebacker, think hand double-team. Two-hand it. Movement is needed to ensure cut-back lane.

CHAPTER 25

ZONE-BLOCKING SCHEMES AND CALLS

Key: OLM = offensive lineman
PSG = playside guard
PST = playside tackle
DLM = defensive lineman
BSG = backside guard
BST = backside tackle

Call: Zebra (across front) C.P. – Call used to direct all OLM to track zone their playside gap. (Used vs. sugar linebackers)	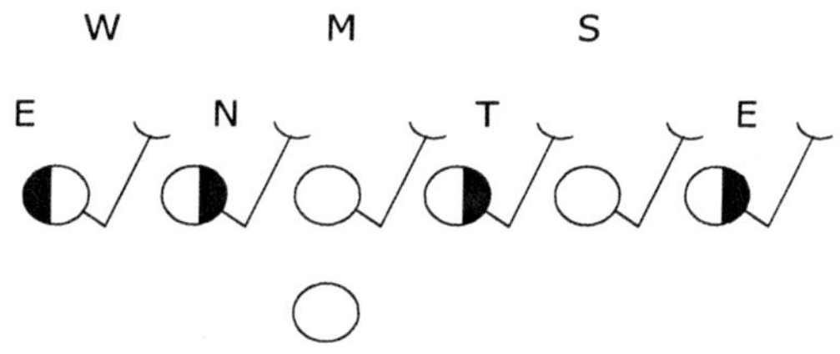
Call: Power zone combo's C.P. – Block involving a covered and uncovered OLM, working in combination to block two defenders; emphasize getting movement on the down lineman and then coming off to block the second-level defender.	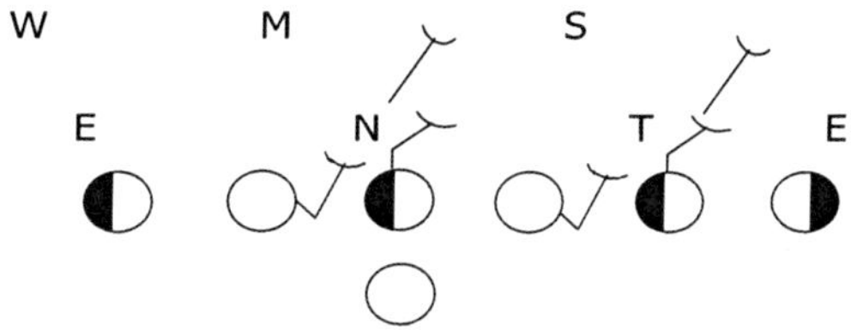
Call: Quick zone combo's C.P. – Block involving a covered and uncovered OLM, working in combination to block two defenders. Emphasize covered OLM to clear DLM to second level quickly; uncovered OLM takes over the down defender on LOS.	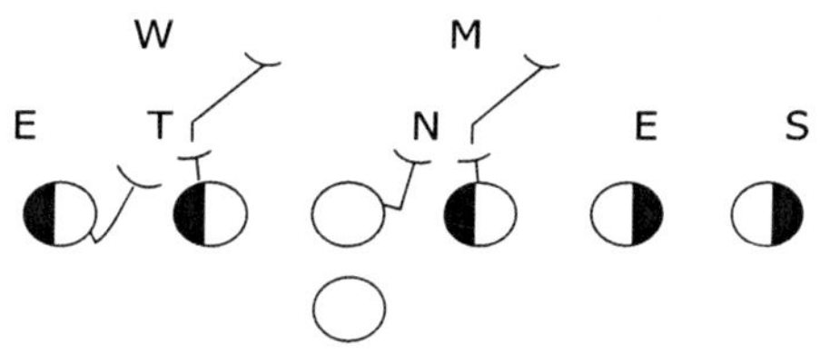
Call: Ace (playside scheme) C.P. – Center and playside guard working together in combination to block #1 DLM to the playside #1 linebacker on the second level. (Power/quick ace)	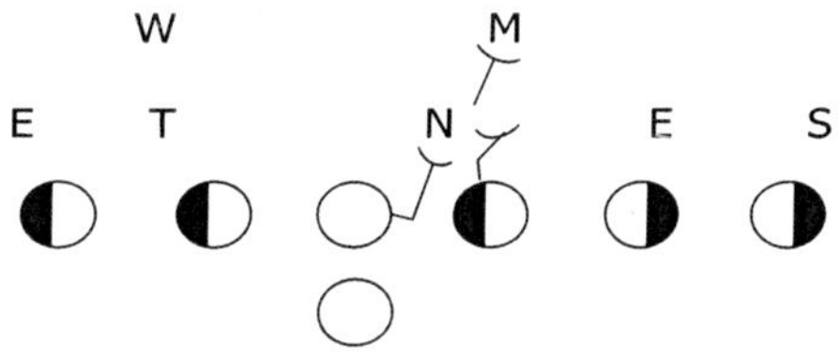

Call: Deuce (playside scheme) C. P. – PSG and PST work together in combination to block #1 DLM to the playside #1 linebacker on the second level. (Power/quick deuce)	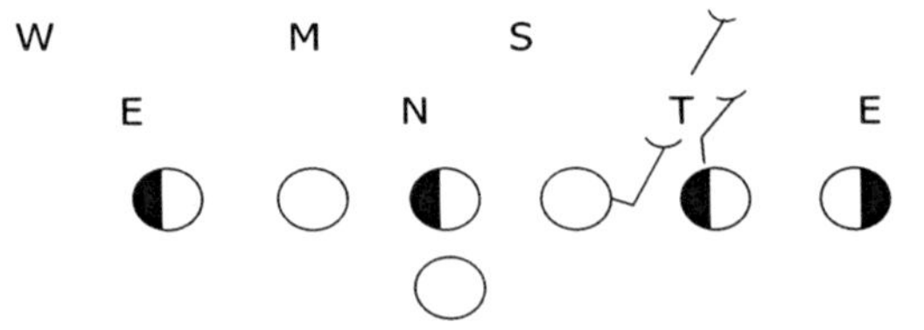
Call: Trey (free safety scheme) C.P. – PST and TE working together in combination to block the #2 DLM to the playside #1 linebacker on the second level.	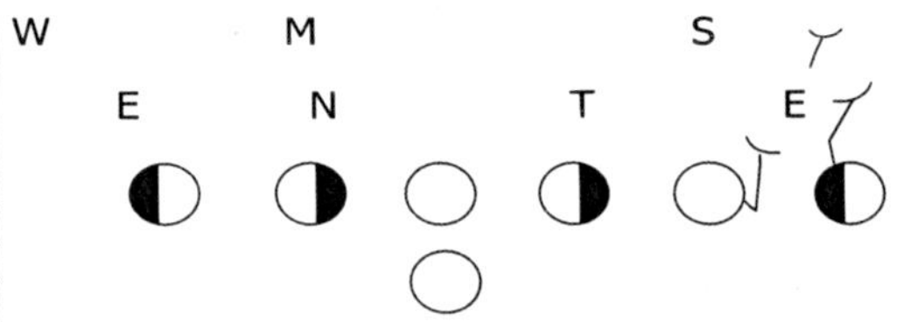
Call: Swipe (backside scheme) C.P. – The center and BSG work together in combination to scoop block the Nose and the #1 linebacker vs. a single linebacker or the Nose and #2 linebacker vs. two linebackers in the box.	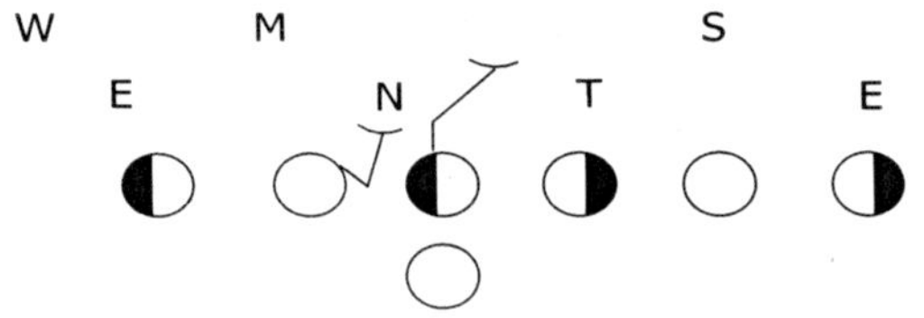
Call: Slip (backside scheme) C.P. – BSG and BST work together in combination to scoop block the backside DLM to the backside #2 linebacker on the second level.	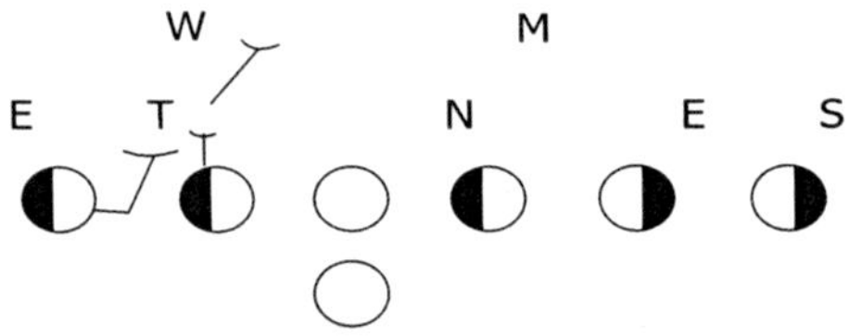
Call: Slide (backside scheme) C.P. – Call by the BSG vs. a 2i-technique, alerts the BST to track zone to #2 backside linebacker. The BSG will block the 2i by himself.	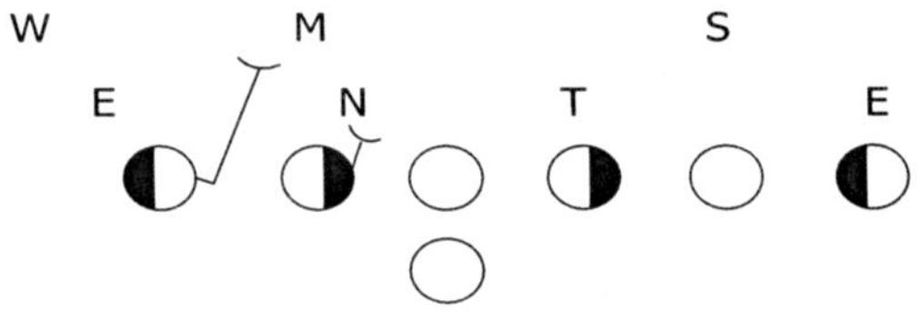
Call: Lock (backside scheme) C.P. – The block made by the BST vs. a 1- or 2-linebacker fronts to block the man on/ outside.	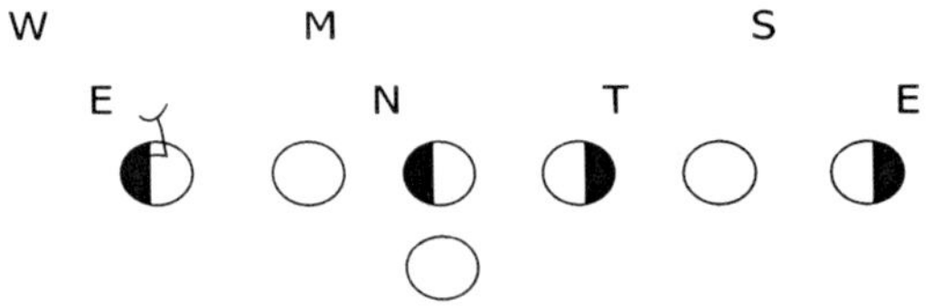

CHAPTER 26

GAP SCHEMES AND CALLS

Key:

OLM = offensive lineman
PSG = playside guard
PST = playside tackle

DLM = defensive lineman
BSG = backside guard
BST = backside tackle

Call: Back (playside scheme)

C.P. – Call made by the center that directs the PSG back to his inside to block the DLM over the center. Center will block the #1 DLM backside over the BSG.

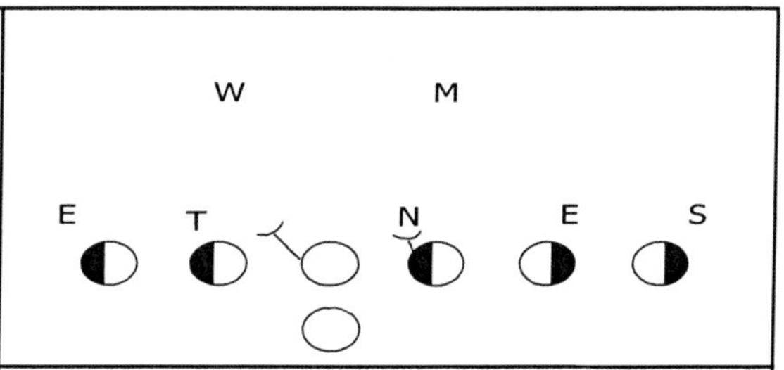

Call: Gin (playside scheme)

C.P. – Block made by the center and the PSG working in combination to block the nose to #2 linebacker. Center lateral steps to the backside A gap. PSG lead steps to the nose and double team the nose to determine who comes off for linebacker.

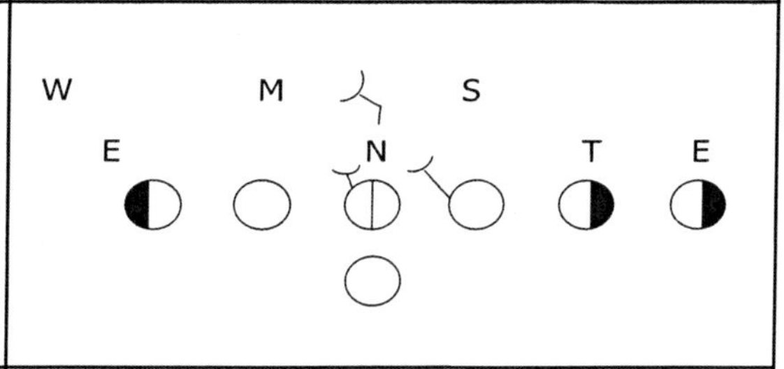

Call: Tag (playside scheme)

C.P. – Block made by PST and PSG working in combination to block the 3-tech to the #2 backside linebacker. PSG lateral steps to the backside A gap. PST lead steps to the 3-tech and double team the 3-tech to the #2 linebacker. Both read the 3-tech to determine who comes off for the linebacker.

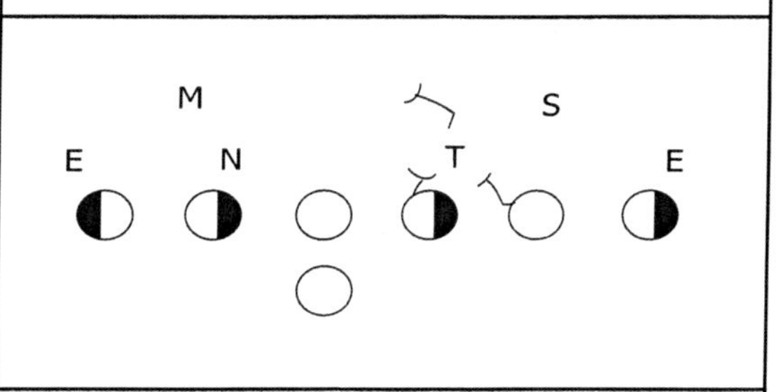

Call: Eat (playside scheme)

C.P. – Block made by PST and TE working in combination to block the 5-tech to the #2 backside linebacker. PST lateral steps to playside B gap. TE lead steps to 5-tech and double teams the 5-tech to #2 linebacker. Both read the 5-tech to determine who comes off for the linebacker.

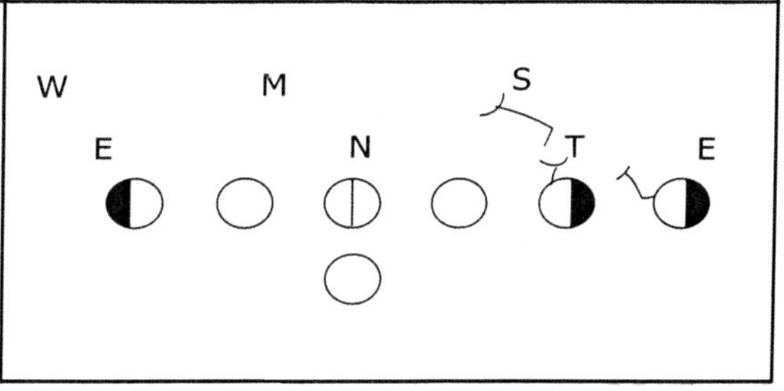

<table>
<tr><td>Call: Macy (playside scheme)

C. P. – Call made by the PST or TE vs. man on with overhang. PST/TE blocks man on. Alert for DE to slant to B gap. Use read step.</td><td>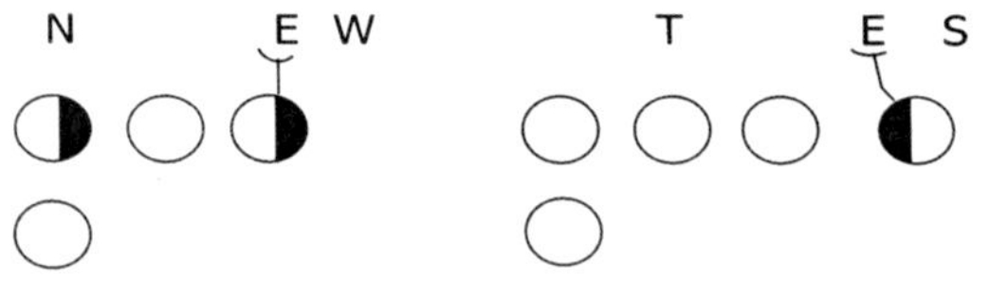
</td></tr>
<tr><td>Call: Gap (playside scheme)

C.P. – Block by the PST vs. 4i-tech; PST gap blocks the B gap defender.</td><td>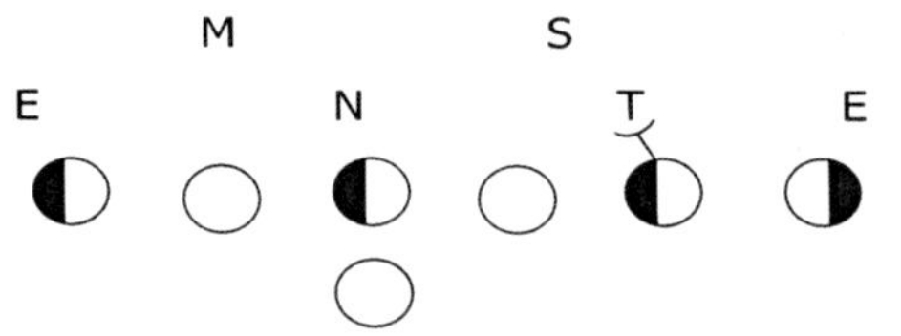
</td></tr>
<tr><td>Call: Gap it (across the front)

C.P. – Call made by the center that directs blockers at the point of attack, to block anyone to their backside gap or the man to their inside.</td><td>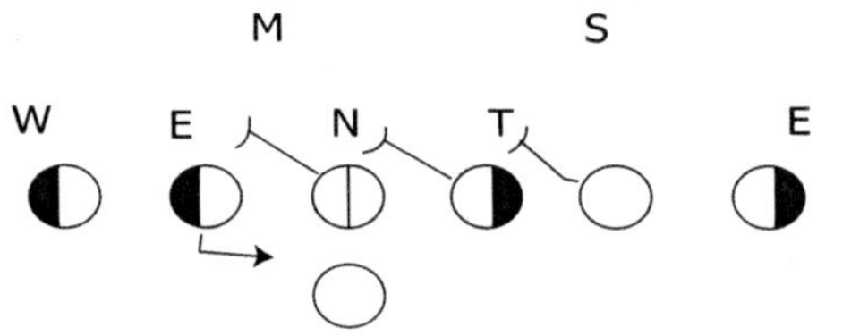
</td></tr>
<tr><td>Call: Smash (backside scheme)

C.P. – Block used by the BST with a 3-tech BST work through 3-tech's backside's hip to second-level #2 linebacker. Used vs. 7-tech over TE.</td><td>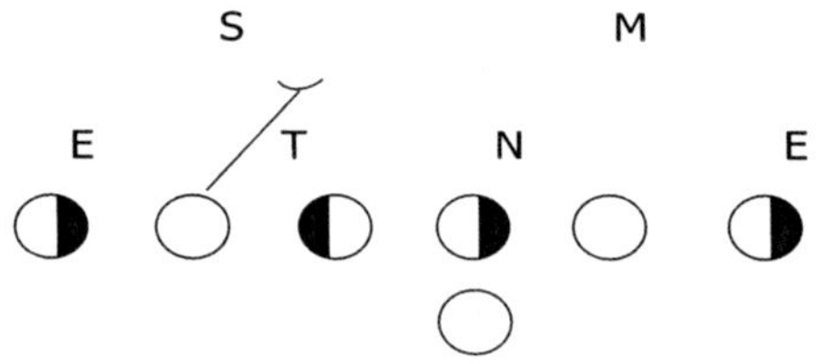
</td></tr>
<tr><td>Call: Me (backside scheme)

C.P. – Call made by the TE vs. a 6/9-tech. Alerts BST to zone seal B gap inside-out. TE will blast inside to cutoff #2 linebacker.</td><td>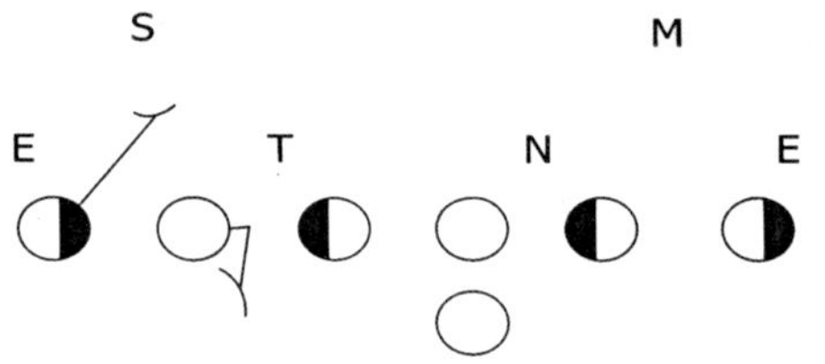
</td></tr>
<tr><td>Call: You (backside scheme)

C.P. – Call made by the TE vs. a 7-tech. Alerts BST to smash to second level to #2 linebacker. TE will cutoff C gap defender; cancels zone seal for BST.</td><td>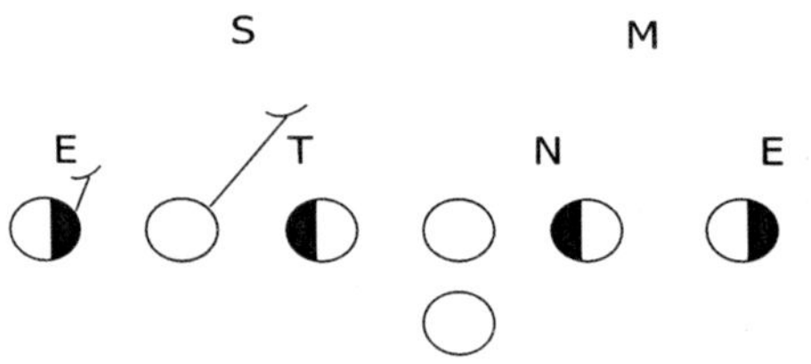
</td></tr>
</table>

Call: Green (backside scheme)

C.P. – Call made by the BSG declaring he will be the puller, pulling playside to block the #1 linebacker. BST executes you/me calls given by TE backside.

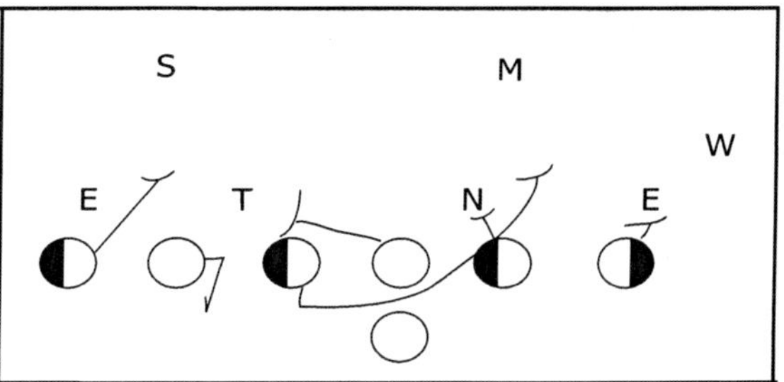

Call: Take (backside scheme)

C.P. – Call made by the BST vs. a 3- or 4i-tech declaring he will be the puller, pulling playside to block the #1 linebacker. BSG blocks 3- or 4i-tech. Center blocks #2 linebacker. TE zone seals C gap.

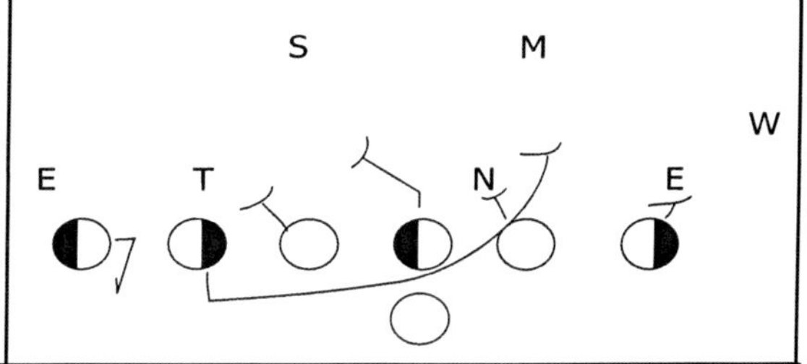

Call: Zone Seal (backside scheme)

C.P. – Blocking technique used by BST. Tackle will take flat lateral step into B Gap & jab with inside hand, taking away defender's inside path, then working back outside blocking end man on the LOS or the level-two fold player.

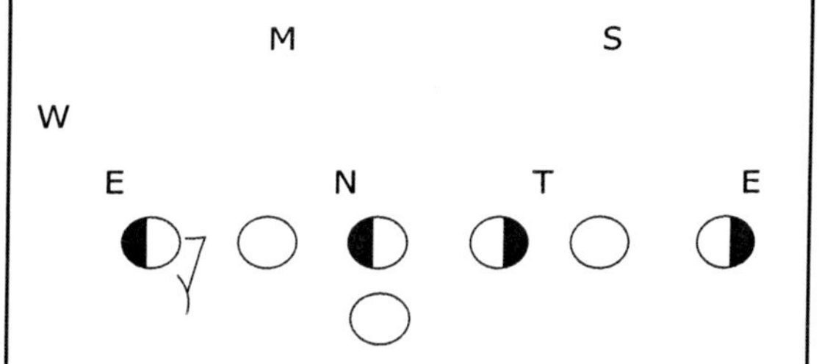

Call: Ed (playside scheme)

C.P. – Call made by playside tackle which alerts the BSG to pull and log/ seal the DE playside. PST uses veer technique to block #1 linebacker.

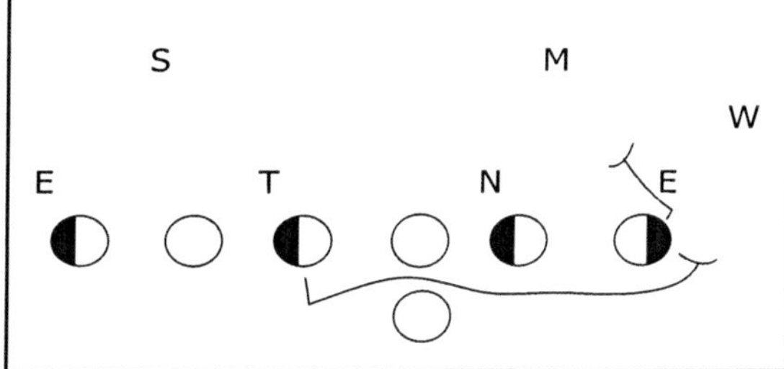

Call: Veer (playside scheme)

C.P. – Block used by the PST on route to #1 linebacker. PST slide steps with outside foot and rip through DE upfield to #1 linebacker playside.

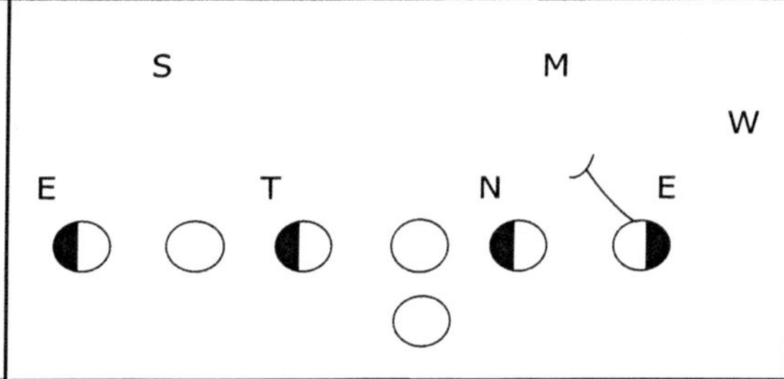

Call: Lead pull (playside)

C.P. – Pulling technique where the BSG takes an open step and pulls down LOS, keeping shoulders square and works up to the second level to block the #1 linebacker playside.

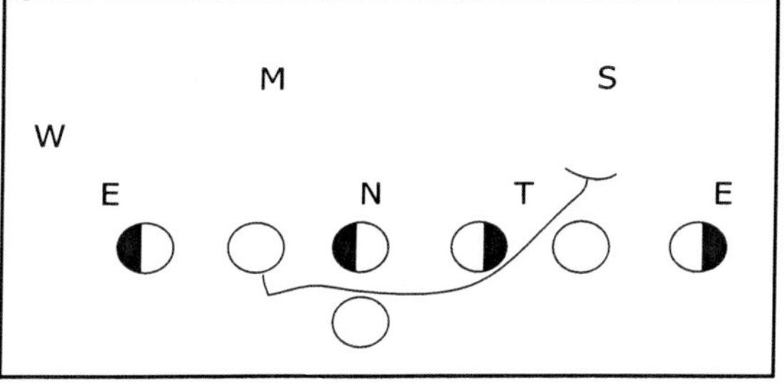

Call: Clip (backside) C.P. – Pulling technique by BST vs. 3 or 4 eye technique. BST open cross step pulls and clips down defender's leg behind the LOS.	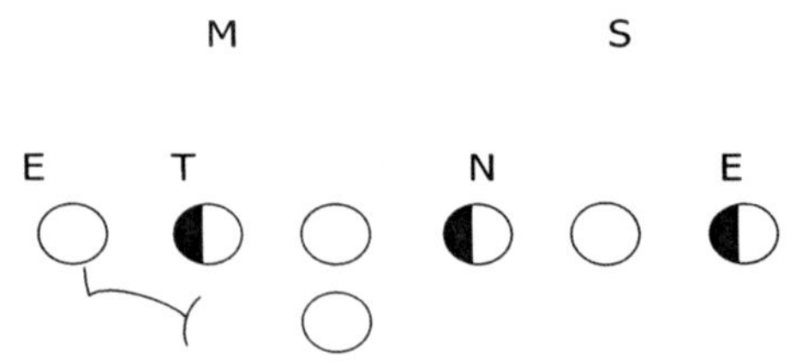
Call: Log/cut pull C.P. – Pulling technique by BSG where he pulls down the LOS playside and reads DE vs. no color upfield. Log DE vs. color upfield. Cut outside thigh board of DE.	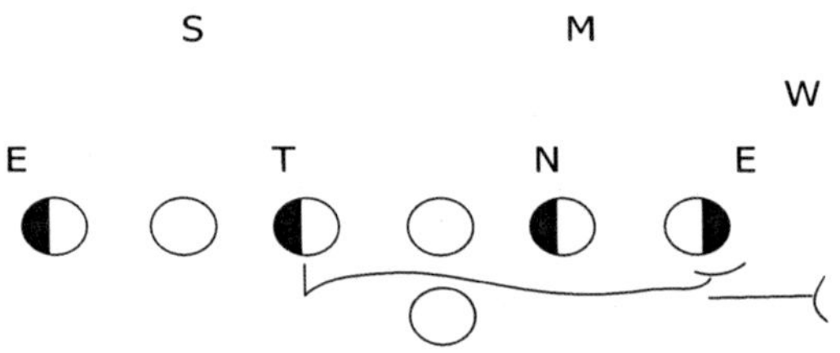
Call: Kickout pull C.P. – Pulling technique by either PSG or BSG where they pull down LOS and kick-out end man on LOS.	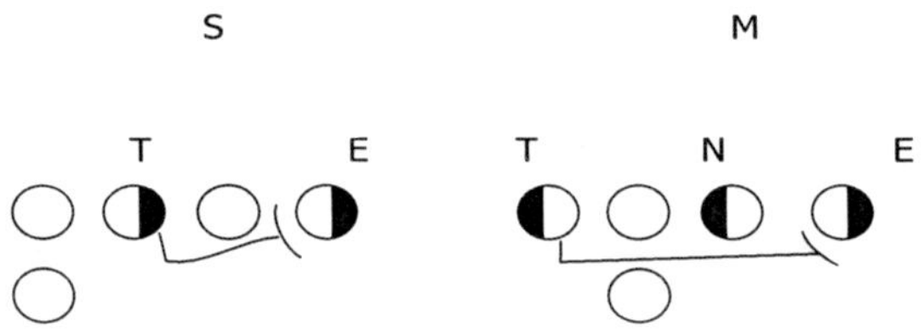

CHAPTER 27

DRAW SCHEMES AND CALLS

Key:

OLM = offensive lineman
PSG = playside guard
PST = playside tackle
DLM = defensive lineman
BSG = backside guard
BST = backside tackle

Call: Bolt (playside scheme)

C.P. – Cross block between the center and BSG vs. weak shade nose or 2i on the backside. <u>Center</u> – step with near foot, drive block near number. <u>BSG</u> – under step with playside foot; step around center block #1 linebacker according to play.

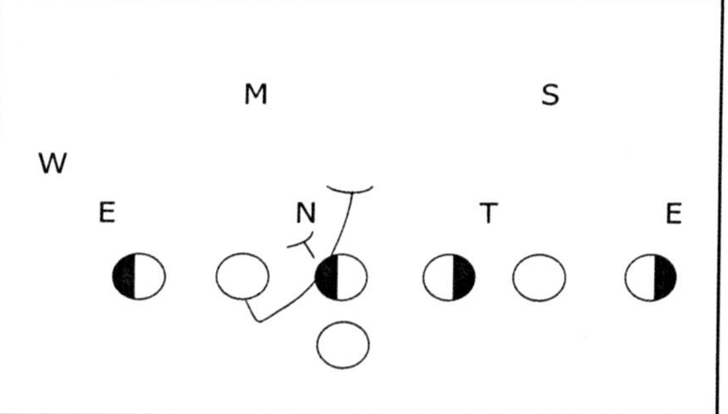

Call: Club (free safety scheme)

C.P. – Cross block between PSG and center vs. strong shaded nose playside. <u>PSG</u> – lead step with near foot; drive block near number. <u>Center</u> – Under step with playside foot; fold around PSG and block playside #1 linebacker (running play only).

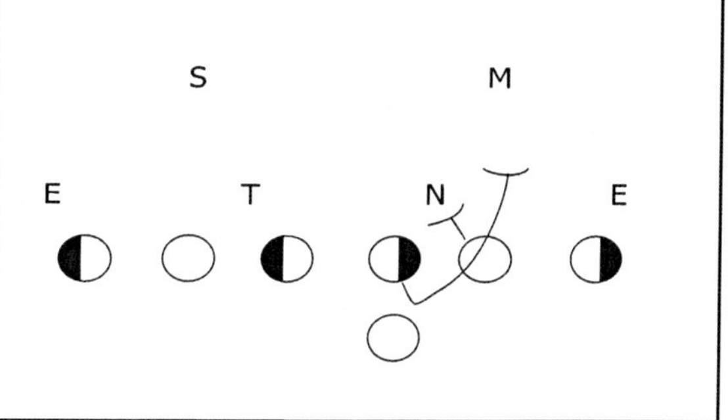

Call: Man (across front)

C.P. – Straight-ahead movement, using a drive block technique if covered by down lineman. If uncovered, lead step and block linebacker.

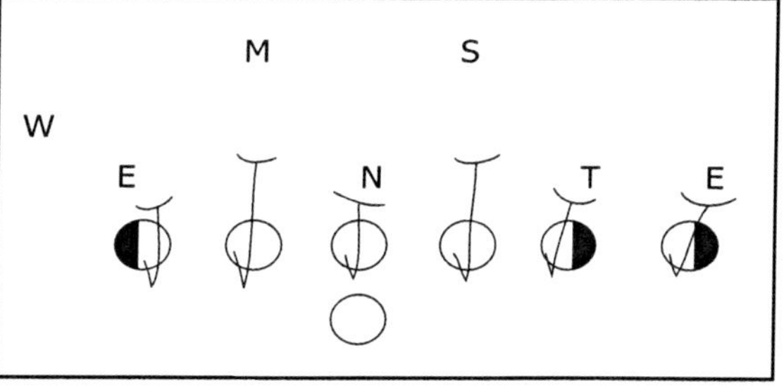

Call: Ted (free safety scheme)

C.P. – Cross block between tackle and TE. Tackle – step with near foot; drive near number. TE – under step w/near foot; step around tackle and block linebacker according to play.

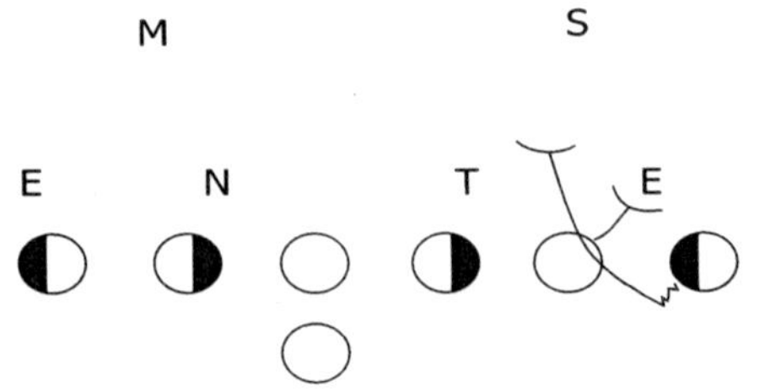

Call: Bob (free safety scheme)

C. P. – Call made by PST alerts PSG to block big-on-big with PST on #1 and #2 defenders on the LOS playside.

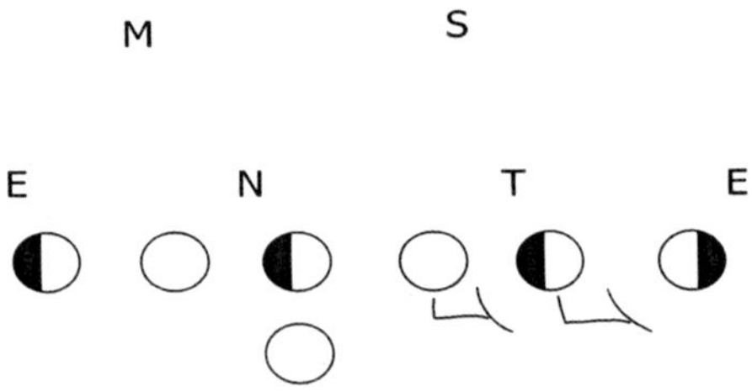

Call: High-wall (backside scheme)

C.P. – Block technique by BST to wall off backside pursuit toward point of attack. Work for position inside out; the tackle builds a wall with his body playside, working upfield to seal off any defender coming from outside second level.

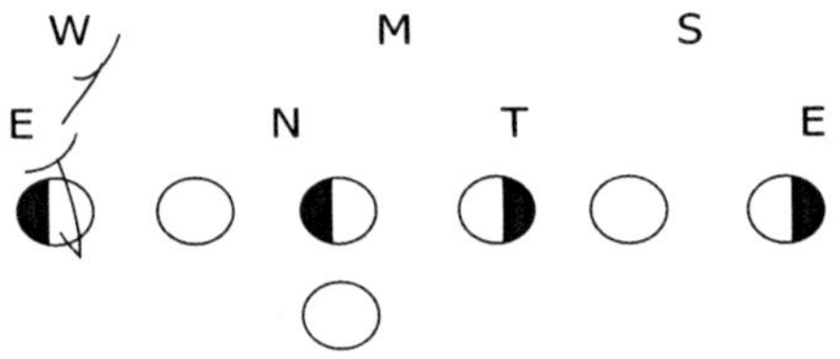

Call: Swap (backside scheme)

C.P. – Call used on backside of draws (cancels bolt call) BST blasts to #2 linebacker; BSG combos with center on nose and comes off to seal DE backside.

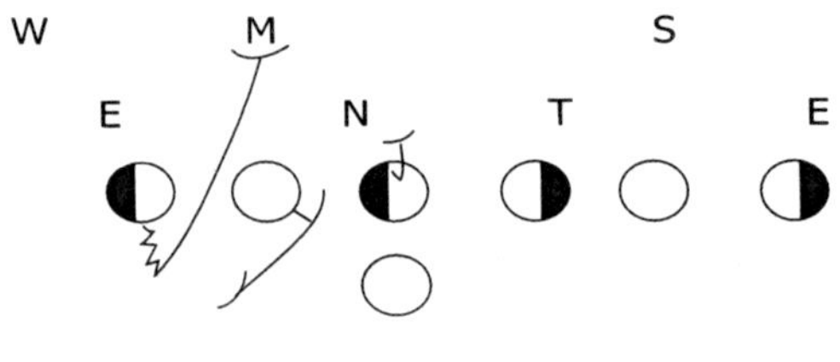

Call: Fan (backside scheme)

C.P. – Call made by the BST vs. man on and overhang. BST blocks the end man on the LOS. BSG blocks #1 DLM.

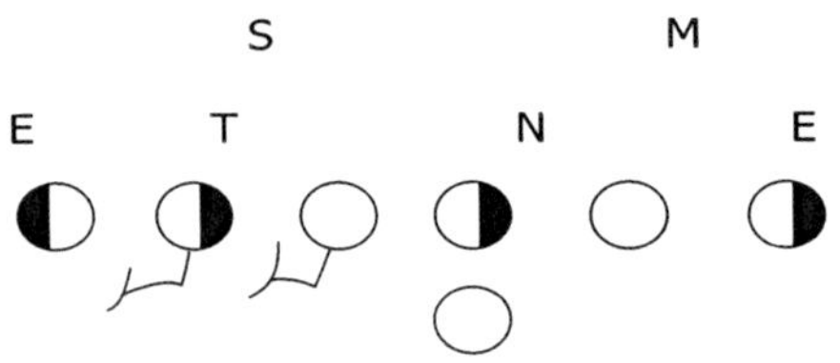

CHAPTER 28

TRAP SCHEMES AND CALLS

Key:

OLM = offensive lineman	DLM = defensive lineman
PSG = playside guard	BSG = backside guard
PST = playside tackle	BST = backside tackle

Call: Long C.P. – Block by the BSG, pulling and trap blocking the end man on the LOS. (5 tech)	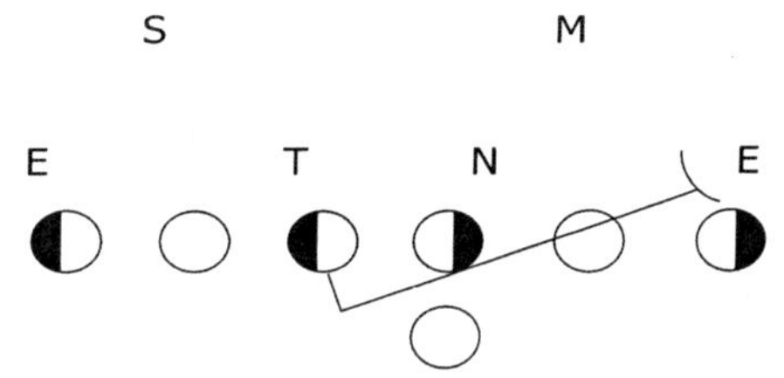
Call: Short C.P. – Block by the BSG, pulling and trap blocking the first down defender past the center (3-tech).	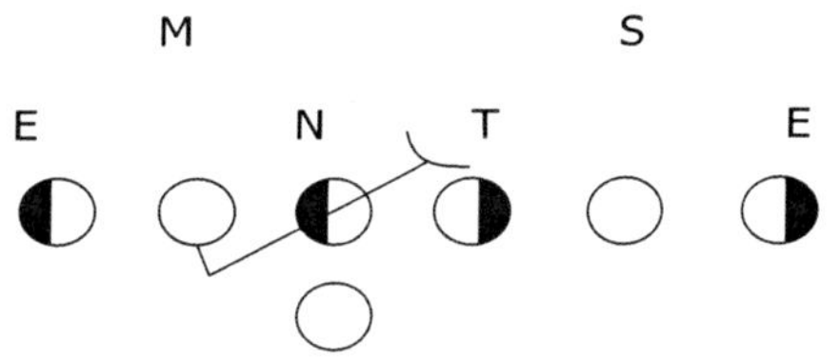
Call: Give C.P. – Call made by the PSG to alert the BSG that he will influence man to be trapped (3-tech).	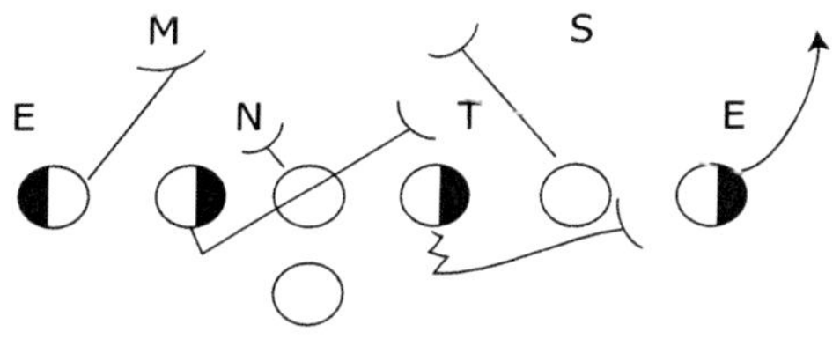

Call: Inside C.P. – Call made by the PSG to alert the BSG that his release will be inside of defender to be trapped.	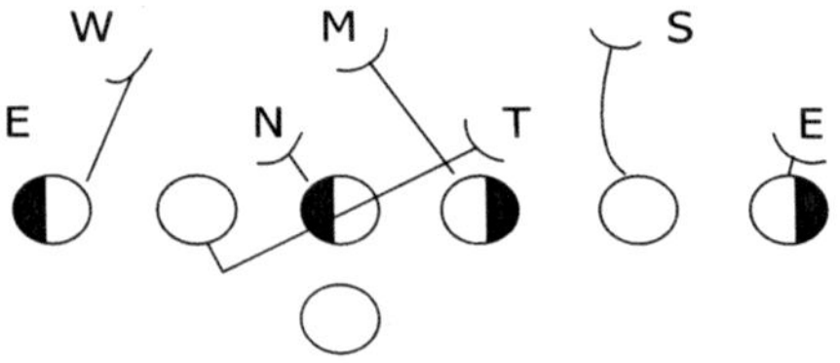
Call: Gas C. P. – Call made by the PSG. PSG will pass set and draw 3-tech upfield and lock on. BSG will "horn pull" and trap near the linebacker.	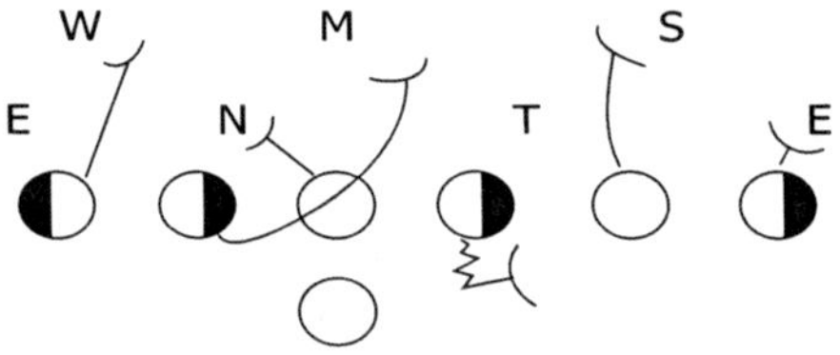
Call: Blast C.P. – Block used by tackle on route to linebackers on trap. Tackles angle lead step with their inside foot clearing level 1 to level 2 quickly to block near linebacker to their inside.	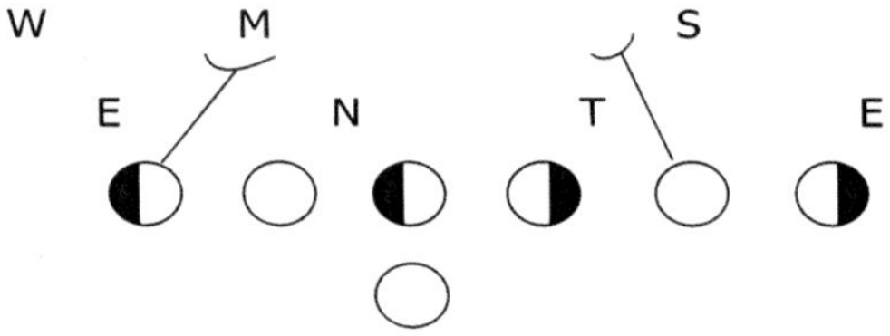

CHAPTER 29

AUXILIARY SCHEMES AND CALLS

Key:		
	OLM = offensive lineman	DLM = defensive lineman
	PSG = playside guard	BSG = backside guard
	PST = playside tackle	BST = backside tackle

Call: Sift C.P. – Block executed by the BST away from the point of attack, blocking backside fold player as he works up and through B gap.	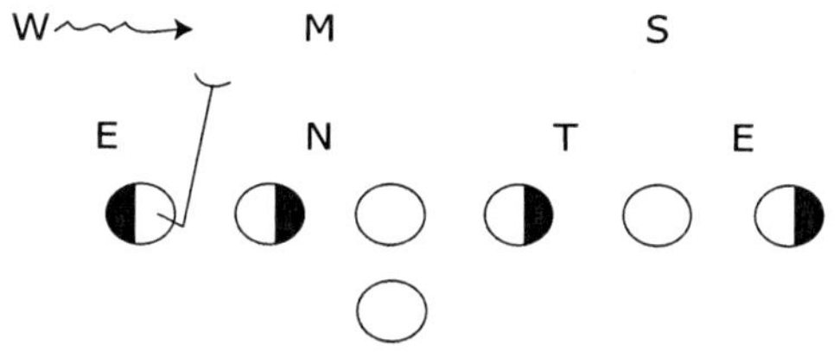
Call: Wedge C.P. – Blocking technique used by OLM. Everyone lead steps to their inside gap and blocks the first threat inside. Center works to nearest shade.	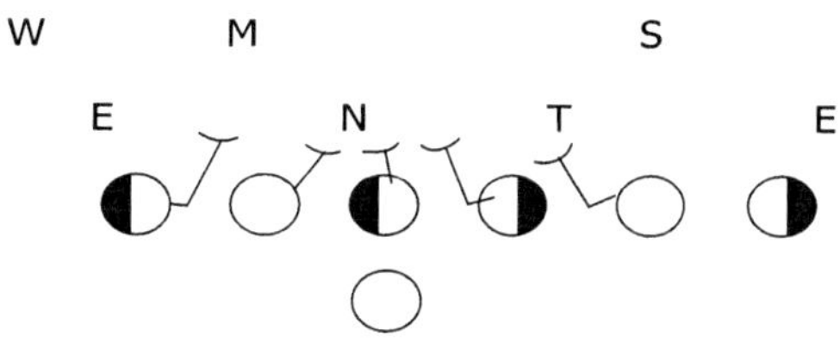
Call: Chip C.P. – Block made by center. Alerts PSG or BSG that the center will chip off their man to the near or backside linebacker.	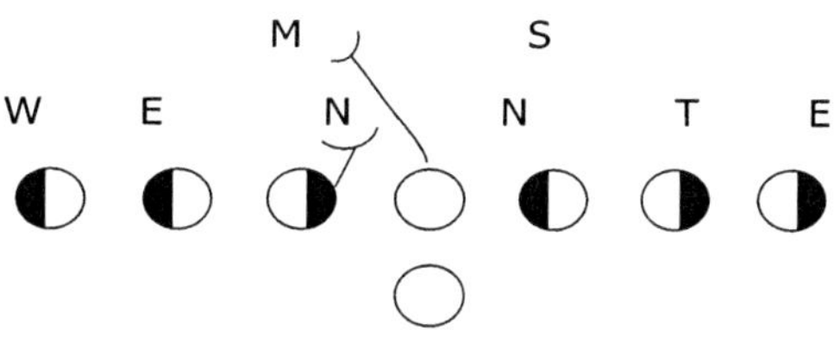

Call: Drape C.P. – Blocking technique used by the backside lineman to reach cutoff through their playside gap (used on goal-line and short-yardage situations).	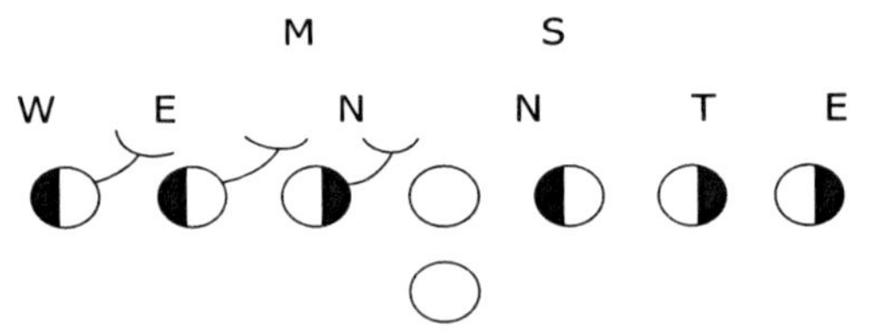
Call: Ace it C. P. – Call made by PSG, directing the center to execute a double team on the #1 defender on the LOS (Used on goal-line and short-yardage situations).	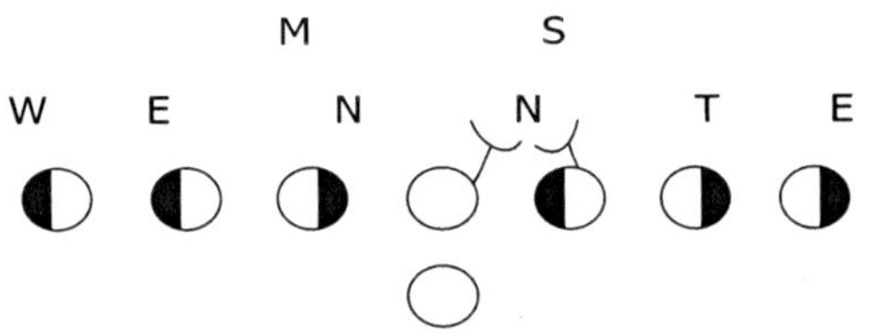
Call: Deuce it C.P. – Call made by PSG, directing the PST to execute a double team on the #2 defender on the LOS (used on goal-line and short-yardage situations).	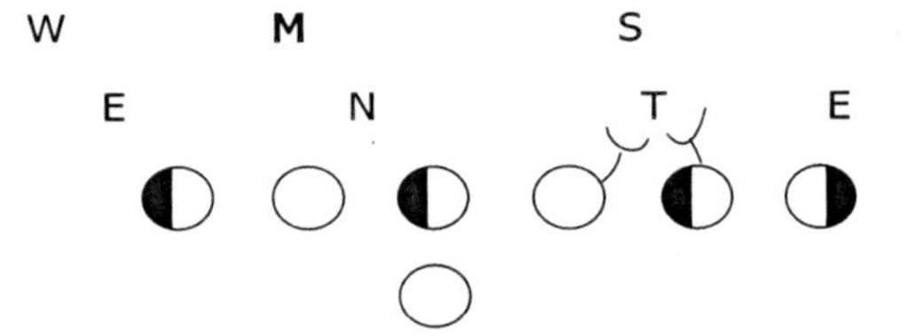
Call: Log/seal C.P. – Block in which the BSG sickle pulls and logs the DE playside on 70/71 sprint-out protection.	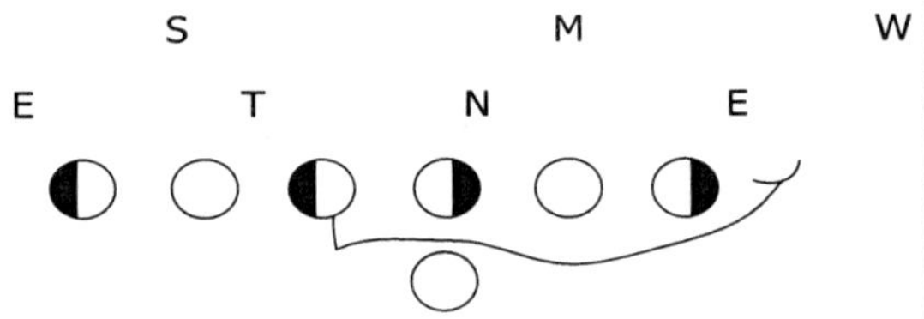
Call: Boot pull C.P. – Block in which the PSG sickle pulls and logs the DE to the boot protection side.	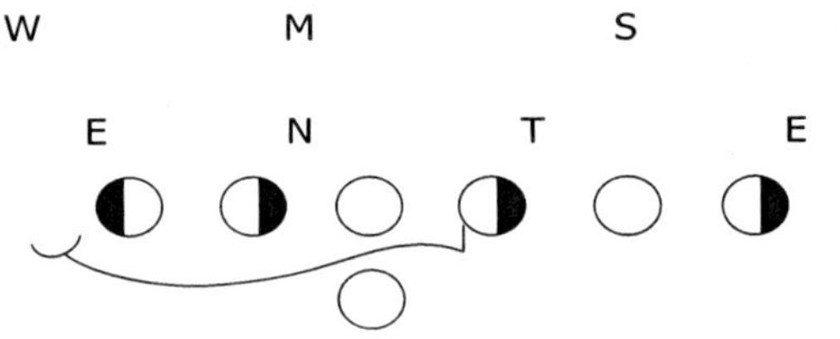
Call: Horn pull C.P. – Pulling technique by the BSG. BSG pulls playside and works to second level to block the playside linebacker.	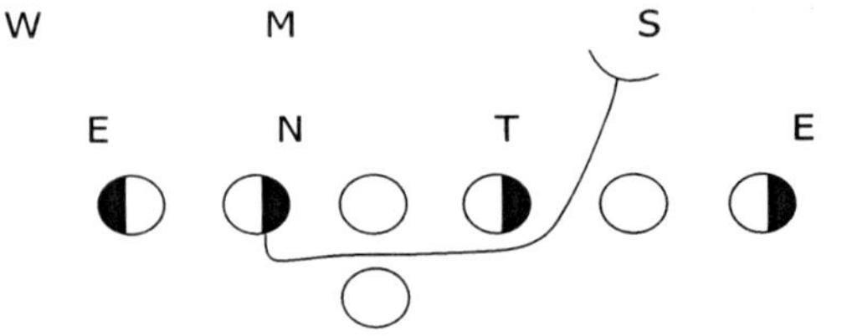

CHAPTER 30

RUN-BLOCKING DRILLS

The drills covered in this chapter are designed to enhance the particular fundamentals, skills, techniques, and segments of the run game. Properly conducted, drill work should achieve the following benefits:

- Improve fundamentals, techniques and skills.
- Teach coordination of the eyes, mind and body.
- Develop confidence and poise.
- Evaluate and determine alignment of personnel.
- Set the tempo for the way the players are going to play the game.
- Create game-like situations in practice.

PRE-PRACTICE DRILL

Recognition Drill. The purpose of this drill is to teach offensive lineman how to recognize and communicate different defensive fronts allowing them to rehearse and execute their assignments. To perform the drill, align six to seven plastic trash barrels, bags, or backup players to represent the defensive alignment. The coach stands behind with scripted plays to review. The offensive line and tight end assume their proper splits, levels, and alignment for the play given on the line of scrimmage. On the coach's snap count, the unit blocks their assignments. (Coaching point: check for proper splits, alignments, stance, footwork, and assignments). Continue the drill until the script is completed and blocked correctly. Vary the drill by changing the defensive looks and alignments.

AGILITY DRILLS

This segment can be used to help linemen work on footwork, quickness, body control, and change of direction and to warm them up prior to practice. The coach should choose a couple of drills to perform daily, depending on the time allotted, or he can change them up daily as a mixer.

- *Duck Waddle.* The purpose of this drill is to enhance the ability of the offensive lineman to maintain a wide base, bending their knees, sinking their hips, and keeping their weight distributed through the insteps of their feet, as they take short power steps with their arms pumping for 10 yards.
- *Quick Corrioca.* The purpose of this drill is to loosen up the hips and work on foot quickness. The emphasis is for the player to stay as low as possible, quickly taking as many steps as he can as he rotates his hips.
- *Four Corners.* The purpose of this drill is to develop foot quickness and change of direction. Place four cones at the corners of a 10-yard by 10-yard square. Players start from a 3-point stance. Mix four different movements to each cone (bear crawl, lateral shuffle, backward run, corrioca).
- *Side Touch.* The purpose of this drill is to help offensive linemen gain flexibility in their hips, maintain knee bend, and improve their ability to follow directional commands. The players face the coach in a good 2-point position with live feet. On the coach's hand direction (right/left), the players react by sinking their hips and knees and placing their directional hand on the ground.
- *Tornado.* The purpose of this drill is to emphasize explosion, foot quickness, body control, and change of direction. The player starts from a 3-point stance, sprints five yards to the first cone, and makes a right-hand turn. He then returns to the starting line, and makes a left-hand turn around the second cone, and sprints five yards and touches the line. He then backpedals across the starting line.
- *Duck Wave.* The purpose of this drill is to teach offensive linemen to bend their knees and sink their hips with a wide base and a solid center of gravity through their midline and the insteps of their feet. They must maintain proper body control as they move and gain ground quickly going forward, backward or laterally to either the left or right. The players start in a good 2-point stance and react to the coach's directional movement. When moving laterally, the player's hand comes up to chest level and moves quickly, simulating pass protection. When moving forward or backward, this arms should be pumping by his side.
- *Zig Zag Wave.* The purpose of this drill is to teach offensive linemen to work angles, change directions, and maintain body control and balance. Players start in a good 2-point stance with their hands up at chest level. On the coach's command, the players execute a kick angle step with their directional foot and slide their backside foot, simulating pass protection footwork first to their right

and then to their left. The emphasis is to keep hands live with a wide base and their shoulders back with their feet in the ground and no body lean.

STANCE AND START PROGRESSION DRILLS

Stance. A lineman should align with an over-wide base slightly wider than the shoulders, with his inside foot up. His knees and toes are slightly ducked out with his weight on the arches of his feet. His weight should be balanced down the midline of his body, with a slight arch in his lower back and his shoulders square. His down hand is slightly extended and placed on the ground with the fingertips in a tripod position. His free hand is either cupped on the side of his knee, or placed on his lower thigh. His eyes are looking through his eyebrows, while focusing on the target.

Setting to the Stance. The lineman assumes a vertical upright position with a toe-to-arch stagger with his feet. On the coach's command, the lineman spreads his feet to an over-wide base. On the next command, the lineman squats into a 2-point position. On the next command, "catch your eyeball," the lineman lifts and cups his down hand to catch his eyeball. The lineman should not shift his body or lose his balance. If either occurs, he is either too heavy-handed or light-handed.

CWM Run/Pass: This drill is done with the entire front five. Initially, the center addresses the ball, and then the guards and tackles follow, setting into their stance. On the coach's command, (run/pass RT/LT), the lineman shifts his weight with his butt. He then fires out, executing proper run footwork or pass sets. (Coaching point: this drill helps the lineman understand how he can shift his weight to execute his techniques and schemes without tipping the defense).

One-Step Starts. The lineman faces five shields or boards placed on the ground which represent defenders. The coach calls out the directional step to be executed. The linemen shift their weight in their stances and execute first step in conjunction with the command "HIT." The linemen hold their position until released. The drill is done quickly to mentally rehearse their techniques of footwork.

Steps Used:

- *Up Field.* Directly forward, with his toes pointed downfield, with his body square to LOS.
- *Angle Lead.* A 45-degree lead step, slightly upfield gaining width.
- *Reach.* A wide lateral, "pick it up put it down", depth step, keeping his hips square, with his shoulders and toes pointed outside.
- *Slide.* A lateral step, with his toes pointed downfield, keeping his hips and shoulders square to the LOS.
- *Drop.* A 45-degree angle depth and width step, opening his hips and shoulders.

- *Open.* A 90-degree open step, with his foot and body corresponding, opening toward the sideline.
- *Under.* Stepping back completely, with his inside foot maintaining his body parallel to the LOS.
- *Crossover.* A 90-degree open step, followed by a crossover step, with his inside foot slightly inside the outside foot to gain depth.

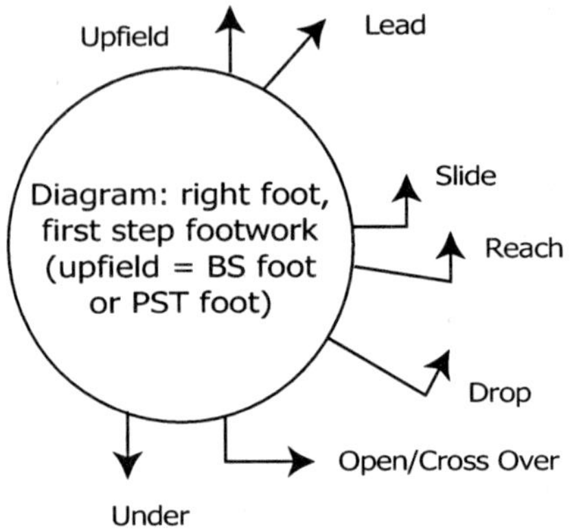

RUN BLOCKING PROGRESSION DRILLS

- *Tracking.* Linemen execute this drill from a 2-point and 3-point stance, incorporating all first steps down the boards on angles. Emphasize base knee bend, power angles, and body control.
- *Bat Drill.* Linemen execute this drill from a 3-point stance, firing out down the chute as their partner swings a bag in their face. Emphasis is to keep eyes open while running and exploding through contact.
- *Lunge/Punch Drill.* Linemen assume a 4-point position on their knees; their toes are curled under their butts, with their arms drawn back and palms of their hands near their hips. On command, the linemen shoot their hands and roll their hips, striking the bag with their thumbs up and their eyes to the sky. Emphasis is to develop hand placement and blow delivery.
- *Fire to Fit.* Linemen execute this drill from a 3-point stance, aligned across from a sled or shield. On command, the linemen execute a proper first step, draw their hands back on second step, explode and shoot their hands with their trail leg into a solid fit position. Their body weight is downhill on the shield, maintaining solid a blocking surface. Emphasis is the importance of blow delivery and exploding the second step. (Coaching point: vary the steps and angles of the bags or boards to incorporate various approaches.)
- *Fit and Finish.* Linemen assume a good 2-point fit position, with their head and eyes in the shield or sled; their thumbs are up and squeezing the shield. Their back is arched with a good wide base and their feet in the ground with their toes slightly pointed out. On command, the blockers explode and snap their

hips, maintaining a wide base, driving up and through the defender's chest, and locking out their arms to finish him off. Emphasis is to teach linemen to accelerate on contact, maintaining leverage, balance and catching their hands with their feet on their follow-through.

- *Full Throttle Drill.* Linemen assume a 3-point stance, aligned across from a defender with a shield or a defender. On command, linemen execute proper first step, firing out, staying low, delivering a blow, maintaining base, and following through to drive and finish the block. Emphasis is to teach linemen to explode off the ball and get movement.
- *Route to Linebackers Drill.* Linemen assume a 3-point stance with their directional foot aligned on the inside corner of the board set at 45-degrees. On command, linemen execute steps given (lead or drop) with outside foot, gaining width, pushing off the inside foot, and maintaining low eye contact as they track down the board while maintaining their base. As the target gets closer, the linemen begin to throttle down and gather themselves by drawing their hands back to strike a blow. Then, they two-hand explode it, working up and through the defender. (Coaching point: they can also incorporate a forearm lift-and-rip to work cutting linebackers).
- *Gather Drill.* Linemen assume a 3-point stance with three shields aligned over them, head up and on right/left 45-degree angles. On command, linemen fire out and block the first defender. The bag holder then releases to the left after being blocked. Linemen then track to the second defender and block him. Then the bag holder releases to the right. Linemen then track to third defender and block him. Emphasis is to coach linemen to maintain center of gravity, sinking their hips and timing their punch, shooting their hands, and accelerating through the defender.
- *Leverage Drill.* A lineman assumes a 2-point fitted position with his partner. The partner places his hands on the blocker's shoulders giving resistance. On command, the blocker drives his partner for five yards. Then, the partner dips and resets his hand into a 2-point fitted position, driving his partner back for five yards. Emphasis is to teach linemen to drop and dip their hips, and shoot their hands, while maintaining leverage base, balance, and follow through.
- *Reach Re-Set Drill.* Lineman assumes a 2-point fitted reach position with his partner. The partner grabs the lineman's outside shoulder and tries to keep outside defensive leverage on the lineman. The lineman rips his outside arm back, resets his head position through the defender's armpit, and rips his inside arm through the defender's outside shoulder, clearing and regaining outside position.
- *Angle Resistance Drill.* Lineman assumes a 2-point fitted reach position with partner. The partner tries to work over the top of the lineman. The lineman presses with his outside hand and shuffles upfield keeping the defender from crossing his face. Lineman must press through the defender's outside leg to sustain leverage.

- *Flipper Drill.* Line assumes a 2-point or 3-point stance across from a shield, aligned on the shoulder of the lineman. On command, lineman works off (up-field/slide) steps and shoots a flipper and his wrist up into the bag on his second step. Emphasis is to keep the flipper tight. The player should be told to "look at his watch to see what time it is."

BLOCKING DRILLS

- *Base Block.* An aggressive man block used at the point of attack. The aiming point is the midline of the defender. Contact occurs on the second step. The length of the first step is determined by the depth of the defender — use a short step if close; take longer step if he is deeper. The timing of the footwork is important using the playside foot. If the defender is head-up or shaded to the lineman's inside, step with the inside foot.
- *Drive Block.* The aiming point is two inches past the midline. The footwork against a head-up or inside-shaded defender is a slide first step and a second step on his inside foot relative to the defender. If the defender slants, he should be taken through his momentum and finished with a strong inside arm if he slants out, and a strong outside arm if he slants inside. (Coaching point: the blocker should not try to stay square to the LOS and should not hesitate or twist his body).
- *Reach Block.* This block is used when the ball carrier runs outside of the blocker. The aiming point is the defender's outside number. The first step is a reach step when the defender is head-up. When the defender is shaded outside, the first step is a drop-step. When the defender is shaded inside, it is a lead-step. The second step is down the crotch. The third step widens the base. The objective of the block is to move the defender, and once outside position is achieved, the blocker locks out his outside arm and works his hips and feet around. (Coaching point: this is not a hook block. The blocker continues to work and maintain an outside position while knocking the defender off the LOS).
- *Down Block.* The aiming point is near the armpit of the defender if he's a reader. If he's a penetrator, the aiming point is the "V" of the neck of the defender. The footwork vs. a loose defender is a slide-step; vs. a tight defender, it is a lead-step. After contact, the blocker should work his outside foot up the field so that the defender is forced underneath, not over the top. If the defender tries to go over the top, he should reverse his shoulders, block him with his outside shoulder, and reverse crab block him.
- *Double Team.* This block is used at the point of attack. The footwork is determined by the alignment of the down defender. Against a head up defender, the covered offensive lineman takes a slide-step with his inside foot and second step just inside the outside foot of the defender. Contact is with his shoulder

and forearm as the blocker attempts to post and lift the defender on contact. The uncovered offensive lineman's first step is a lead-step with his inside foot. The aiming point is the "V" of the neck of the defender. If the defender plays straight, both linemen block the defender upfield, getting ready to come off for the backside linebacker. If the defender slants inside, the covered lineman two-hands it and locks on the defender, as the uncovered lineman works upfield to level two to block the linebacker. If the defender slants out, then the covered lineman powers up to the linebacker.

Against an outside shade, the covered lineman takes an inside, upfield step, driving his shoulder and forearm into the inside number of the defender. The reads of the defender's reaction are the same for a head-up defender. The uncovered lineman takes a slide-step with his inside foot. Against an inside shade, the defender is treated as a head-up defender who has slanted to the inside. The footwork is the same as when the defender is head-up.

PULLING TECHNIQUES

- *Short Trap.* The footwork for a short trap is an open-step with the playside foot and a pivot off the backside foot. The lineman takes a course for the near shoulder of the defender. This action will force the lineman to work up and into the LOS as he pulls. The defender is trapped with the outside shoulder and forearm. On all traps, if the defender penetrates upfield into the backfield, the blockers should not adjust his course. He should turn up to the second level for the linebacker.
- *Fold Block.* The fold block involves a down block by the uncovered lineman, with the covered lineman folding around for a linebacker. The fold blocker takes an under step and shuffles around the down block, keeping his shoulders square with a wide base. The aiming point on the linebacker is the outside number.
- *Sweep.* A sweep involves a guard or tackle pulling to block a linebacker on an outside play. The lineman pulls for a course deep off the LOS and reads the block of the tight end. If the puller can get outside the tight end, then he skins around, blocking the outside number of the linebacker. If the tight end's block widens, he then plants off his outside foot and turns up in the hole and base blocks the linebacker. The footwork used is an open-step.
- *Power.* The power play using a gap scheme playside involves a fullback kicking out the end man on the LOS, with the backside guard pulling for the playside linebacker. The footwork of the backside guard is an open-step with his shoulders and hips facing the sideline. As he pulls, he reads the fullback's block on the end man on the LOS. If he kicks him out, the backside guard turns up inside and base blocks the linebacker. If the defender wrong arms the fullback, the fullback logs the defender. The backside guard then leads around the fullback and blocks the scraping linebacker's outside number.

- *Counter.* The counter play uses a gap scheme playside with the backside guard and backside tackle pulling playside. The backside guard pulls, using an open-step flat down the LOS with his shoulders and hips facing the sideline. If the end man on the LOS is on or across his path, the lineman kicks him out. If the defender wrong arms him, the lineman logs/seals the defender. The backside tackle pulls, using an open cross-step to gain depth (with his backside foot splitting the guard's crotch). He should read the relationship of the end man to the LOS relative to the guard's course before the actual block. Otherwise, the tackle is late. If he kicks him out, the backside tackle turns up inside and base blocks the linebacker. If the defender wrong arms the backside guard, the backside tackle will lead around the backside guard and block the scraping linebacker's outside number.
- *Clip.* The clip is a backside cut technique used to chop down a backside chasing defender behind the LOS. The footwork is an open-step and crossover with the playside foot getting depth. This technique allows the defender to get upfield and pursue. The lineman then clips the back of the defender's legs as he pursues. This method is used on the backside by the tight end and backside tackle when the ball is run outside.

ZONE BLOCKING

Zone blocking involves the lineman blocking his defender unless the defender plays into the blocker who is working with the lineman in combination. Zone blocking is all about staying on tracks. The lineman who is covered by a down defender never changes, always making contact on his second step. The uncovered lineman generally makes contact on his third step on his course through the down defender's alignment to the linebacker.

When the two linemen come together at the down defender, this area is referred to as the "junction point." An *outside* read is when the down defender works outside. The covered lineman continues to push, while the uncovered lineman punches with his outside hand at the down defender, and then tracks up to the linebacker. An *inside* read refers to the down defender working inside. On this read, the uncovered lineman places his outside hand on the ribs or back of his partner and presses him off, allowing him to come off and work for the linebacker. Once the covered blocker has released, the down defender is two-handed by the uncovered lineman. A *gray area* read involves the fact that the down defender is engaged with the covered lineman and is hanging tough inside. This read tells the uncovered blocker to take his outside hand and push on the near shoulder of the down defender and drive him back into the linebacker. The covered lineman stays on the down defender as they work together, getting movement on the down defender to the linebacker.

TYPES OF ZONE COMBOS

- *Power Zone.* This zone combination is used when the running back's course is the hole to cutback. The lineman wants to get movement on the level-one defender first, letting the running back's flow help in blocking the linebackers. The covered lineman uses a drive block technique. On the drive-block, contact is made on the second step. If the defender plays straight, then the blocker continues to get upfield movement. If the defender slants inside, then the blocker gathers his feet, staying square until he feels pressure in his ribs or his back from the uncovered lineman. This pressure tells him to release through the defender to the linebacker. If the defender slants out, then he locks and takes his momentum driving the defender outside. The uncovered lineman executes his junction point-reads on his third step. His landmark is two inches past the down defender. His first step is a drop-step, which opens his body with depth at his landmark. It is important that the uncovered lineman is deeper than the covered lineman so he can read the defender properly, without the combination getting split. The second step is a short-step that should never crossover beyond the blocker's own hip. The third step widens his base, and the blocker executes the junction point reads.

- *Quick Zone.* This zone combination is used when the running back's course is outside the combination block. The lineman tries to get to the second level quickly. The covered lineman uses a reach block. He stays on the block unless the defender slants to the inside. When this happens, the covered lineman gathers his feet while maintaining the same track to block the flowing linebacker. It is important for the lineman to stay underneath the linebacker and not shoot so far down field that the linebacker runs underneath. The uncovered lineman aims for the space past the shoulder of the defender. The idea is to scoop the covered blocker off for the linebacker. When scooped off (hand in the ribs), the playside hand goes for the shoulder of the defender to hook him. The uncovered blocker always uses a three-step course through his landmark and executes the junction.

- *Swipe Combos.* These blocks are backside scoops, which can be either power or quick scoops, depending if it is an inside or outside zone play. The covered lineman executes an upfield step with his backside foot and a second step tracking at 45-degrees. His backside hand punches or forearm flippers through the defender's inside half, trying to turn the defender's shoulders open. If the down defender slants inside, the lineman two-hands it and locks on him down the track. The uncovered lineman drop-steps, with his aiming point at the down defender's inside armpit. Contact occurs on the third step. The lineman pushes the covered lineman with his playside hand and takes over the down defender. If the down defender disappears inside, the lineman continue on track to block the linebacker.

GROUP DRILLS

- *2-on-2 / 3-on-3.* Work combinations of frontside and backside blocks (vs. no flow, vs. flow, vs. slant, vs. angle)

  √ Base/drive block √ Pulls √ Double team

  √ Reach block √ Frontside zone combos

  √ Down block √ Backside zone combos

- *Full-Line Schemes.* Work vs. base fronts, stems, stunts, blitz, and sugar walked-up linebacker.

  √ Zones √ Counter √ Option

  √ Toss √ Draw

  √ Power √ Iso's

SECTION III

PASS BLOCKING

Philosophy of Pass Protection

The Ten Commandments of Pass Protection

Fundamentals of Pass Protection

Pass-Protection Components

Pass-Protection Movements

Pass-Protection Techniques

General Line Pass Terminology

Pass-Protection Drills

CHAPTER 31

PHILOSOPHY OF PASS PROTECTION

PASS PROTECTION is often the offensive lineman's greatest challenge. It is a skill that requires patience and individual concentration, combined with total effort. These qualities are more vital in the passing game than in any other phase of football. From a psychological standpoint, good pass protection is paramount to offensive confidence and success. From a technical standpoint, it is the most difficult to master of any technique. However, perfection can be achieved by any lineman who has reasonable physical ability, pride, and desire and exerts the effort to be the best.

In order to become a good pass protector, it is essential that linemen exhibit knowledge of the following:

- The pass offense and variations of pass protection.
- The opponent's defensive scheme and individual tendencies.
- How to apply the proper techniques on situation passing.
- The type of protection that goes with each call and the adjustments.
- The position from where the ball is thrown (QB Set Point).
- The timing of all passes — whether it requires maximum protection or whether aggressive blocking is indicated.
- The techniques involved in play-action, nakeds, boots, roll and screen passes.

Pass protection should allow a lineman to be *"PHYSICAL"*. You should look for controlled aggression in your pass protectors. Being passive is not allowed.

Pass protectors should be *ACCOUNTABLE* for their performance. Their goal should be a "protection shutout." Their focus should be on the following:

No Mental Busts

No Penalties

No Sacks

No Pressures/Knockdowns

No Batted or Deflected Balls

Coaching point: it is important that linemen study film. They should look at a defender's rush tendencies. It is critical to know an opponent's counter moves, inside or out, and how many steps he takes before making his move. They should look for key tendencies such as twist alerts, cheated alignments, change of stance, weight distribution, etc.

CHAPTER 32

THE TEN COMMANDMENTS OF PASS PROTECTION

1. Know your assignment, split, and alignment.
2. Know the quarterback set-up point on each protection.
3. Know your sets and technique vs. all alignments.
4. Never miss an automatic or line call.
5. Set quickly and strong. Make your stand on the line of scrimmage.
6. Do not allow inside penetration. Never get beaten inside on man protection.
7. Never take an outside fake. Always respect an inside fake. Always anticipate the rusher's second move and counter accordingly.
8. Shuffle for positioning. Always keeping one foot on the ground,. Do not cross your feet. Keep your base. Maintain a slightly inside-out position on the defender.
9. Finish your job. Keep the rusher away from the quarterback.
10. Refuse to be beaten.

CHAPTER 33

FUNDAMENTALS OF PASS PROTECTION

TEMPO:

- Set up in one motion.
- Set on the move.
- Base your set on the defender's alignment.
- Dictate attitude and establish your position on the man.
- Set with speed and quickness.
- Beat the rusher to the set-up spot.
- Prevent oversetting in slide and man.

TARGET:

- Get your head and eyes on the target.
- Sight adjust the landmark to give you leverage.
- Anticipate the initial and the second move.
- Concentrate; look the target in.
- Maintain your position on the rusher.
- Your eyes lead the body; draw your eyes in.
- Proper target allows you to keep a relative position between the rusher and the quarterback.
- Honor inside moves; dishonor outside fakes.

FOOTWORK:

- Coordinate your hands and feet; carry your feet under your hips; your hips are tied to your knees.
- Keep your center of gravity down.
- Be an athlete and a kneebender.
- Keep a wide base and maintain balance and body control.
- Give ground grudgingly.
- Have a foot-pressure demeanor in order to re-direct.
- Cover the rusher up, nose-to-nose, toes-to-toes.

PUNCH:

- Develop a decisive punch.
- Stop the initial charge.
- Deliver your hands under and up for a leverage lock-out.
- Strike your punch on the move as close to the line of scrimmage as possible.
- Force the rusher to re-start, re-direct and re-separate.
- Create separation by re-starting, re-fitting, and re-sinking to get back to balance.
- Don't come off your legs on contact; keep leverage in your legs with your shoulders square.
- Thumbs in front of your eyeballs.
- Drive your thumbs to the defender's sternum.
- Snap your wrists and elbows.
- Patience and timing are the key, you must develop poise.
- Snap a punch and lockout.

FINISH:

- "*IT AIN'T OVER TILL IT'S OVER.*" Don't cut anyone loose! Help violently. Scan or finish rusher as far away from quarterback as possible. Compete and battle your rear end off!!
- Maintain a relative position for the interval.
- Follow; do not pull your arms or hands out.

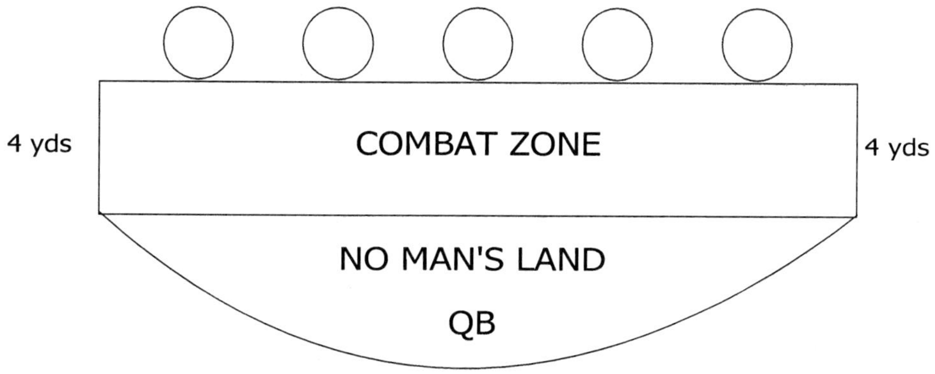

CHAPTER 34

PASS-PROTECTION COMPONENTS

I believe in a staggered power position with the pass-protection blocker's inside foot up. His weight is on his inside foot with his back straight and his head back. The blocker has good power angles in his hips, knees and ankles with his outside foot back. If a picture of defender is taken, his thumbs are together and his elbows are flexed, and pointed at the chin of defender. This is called a post-stagger position and is basic. Offensive linemen need to maneuver comfortably in this position. All of their weight should be over their inside foot. The following points should be kept in mind:

POSTURE:	The duck (a fundamental football position).
FEET:	Get down by width; toe it out, knock-kneed.
POST FOOT:	Inside foot; hold your weight inside on the post.
KICK FOOT:	Outside foot.
KNEES:	Bend at the knees, not at your waist (squat); knees forward, knock-kneed.
BACK:	Keep your back at a 30-degree angle; show the defender your numbers (i.e., your shoulders are back).
SHOULDERS:	Square, "square as much as you can for as long as you can"; don't get grabbed; square to the defender (relative position).
HANDS:	Maintain carriage at chest level; "feelers"; keep your hands and elbows inside; have loose hands; be ready for swats, grabs.
HEAD:	Tuck the chin in; don't get grabbed.

CHAPTER 35

PASS-PROTECTION MOVEMENTS

QUICK SET:	An aggressive set on the LOS into duck set.
SOFT POST:	A one-foot set with the inside or outside foot.
HARD POST:	Aggressive lateral inside set with the shoulders square. (shuffle/shuffle).
DROP SET:	Outside foot depth set and slide inside foot straight back, giving ground to time your set.
POWER SET:	Never have both feet off the ground; always two steps for reaction.
KICK ANGLE:	Explode to gain ground; kick and slide for width.
DEEP DROP:	Explode for depth, and then kick and slide for width.
SLIDE:	Aggressive lateral movement, keeping pads square on the line of scrimmage.
ELEPHANT:	Attack up and in line of scrimmage with an arm swing.
SEPARATION:	Recoil; get man off you.
BASE SET:	Duck set with your back straight; your hand, elbows, and head side frame with your weight inside your ankles.
CORK SCREW:	Point of no return.
RESET:	Regain hand position.
CLUB:	Arm check; get hands off you.
COUNTER:	Redirection on outside/inside move.
JUMP SET:	Quick controlled set, followed by an aggressive jump set, jarring the defender's chest as you attack upfield.
COVER:	Sprint to the football after it has been released from the quarterback.

CHAPTER 36

PASS-PROTECTION TECHNIQUES

GUARDS — SET-UP

The set-up used is based on the defender's alignment on the lineman. The lineman must beat the rusher to the set-up spot. He should determine where the set-up spot is going to be, not the rusher. If he is not set (i.e., knees bent, head up, with arms in a strike position,) he is in early trouble.

Diagram: Guard set-up

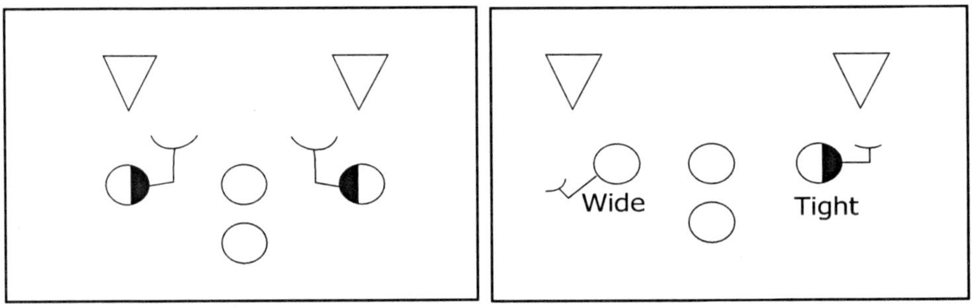

1-TECH SET (HARD POST)

3-TECH SET (SOFT POST–Tight Shade)
(DROP SET —Wide Shade)

TACKLES — SET-UP

The set up used is based on the defender's alignment on them. With the defensive end in a wide position, the tackle should kick to his set-up by moving his outside foot first. With the defensive end in a heads-up position, he should move his inside foot first. He must beat the rusher to the set-up spot. He must be set firmly in the ground. His set-up spot will vary with the defensive end's original alignment, and is a position that takes away his straight line to the throwing spot. His position will be slightly inside-out, giving him a position to cover the entire man from inside out.

Diagram: Tackles set-up

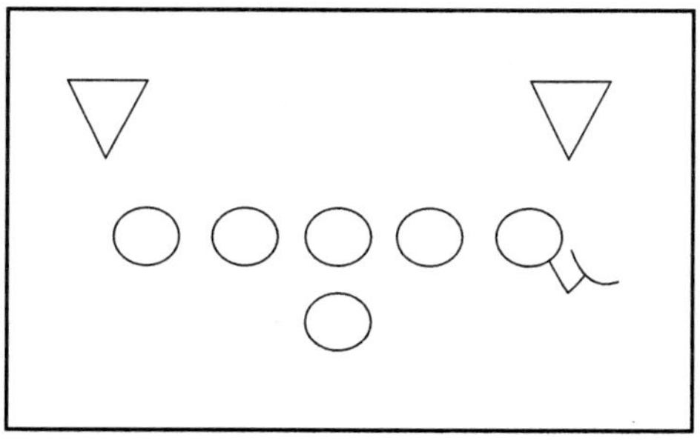

5-TECH SET (DROP SET)

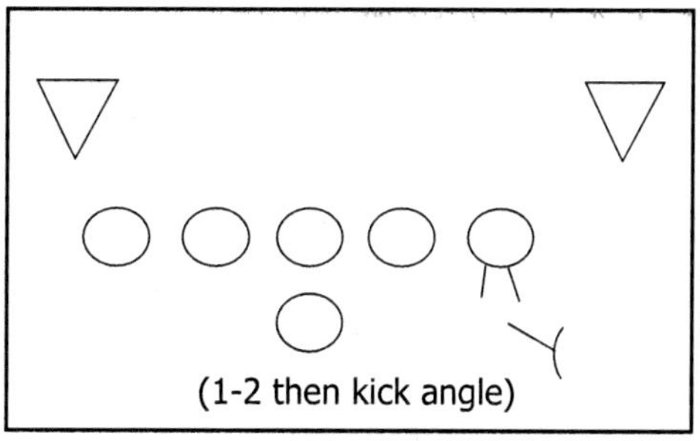

WIDE 5-TECH SET (KICK ANGLE)

GUARD AND TACKLES — CONTACT

Perfect contact is made with the lineman's body position square to the rusher or slightly inside. He should focus his eyes on the rusher's number. His knees are bent, his head is up, his arms are extended but not locked, and his elbows are in the palms-open position. From this position, he will engage the rusher. Contact should be made with his hands. This contact is a "jam", with the target on either side of the rusher's number. A successful "jam" will cause the rusher to be stopped and re-direct this charge. On delivery, his knees will extend, but not lock. His hips will roll forward and up, providing power for the "jam". His arms will lockout, with his elbows pointing downward. He should never make contact with his helmet.

GUARDS AND TACKLES — FINISH

After the initial "jam", one of two things will occur. If his "jam" has been successful, he will disengage from the defender. He should immediately return to the set-up position and prepare for contact again. If the "jam" has been less than 100% successful, (i.e., contact remains from the defender's grab or body push), he should widen his base, work for maximum knee bend, and "bench" him quickly. He needs to work to get his hands inside his hands and establish a "jam". He should never have his arms locked out.

PASS-PROTECTION TECHNIQUE AGAINST DEFENSIVE LINE GAMES AND BASIC LINEBACKER DOGS

Rules of the Technique:

- Anticipate a game, but never guess.
- Never pass until you "feel" your adjacent teammate, and he forces the switch.
- Never get your head "in there" on the initial set-up.
- Always keep a 90-degree angle in your knees.

BASIC FOOTWORK

To fully understand pass protection sets and how to move his feet, the lineman should be aware that he should move to his sets based on the defender's technique.

FOOT STAGGER. The basic premise of the foot stagger is to always keep a foot staggered. The inside foot is the post foot, while the outside foot is the kick-step. Linemen on the left should be in a left-handed stance with their left or set kick-step foot back. Their right foot or post foot should be up. The linemen on the right side are in a right-handed stance. Their right foot is their set kick-step foot, and their left foot is their post foot.

Left Guard/Tackle Stance   Right Guard/Tackle Stance

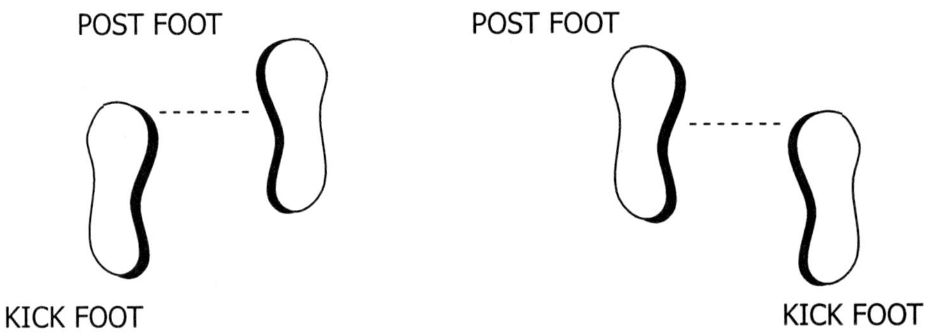

PASS PROTECTION SET VS A 2-TECHNIQUE (HEAD-UP DEFENDER)

The feet do not pump in place vs. a man, a head-up or on a straight rush. The set foot will jam into place and pump if the defender doesn't get up into you right away. This technique is typically employed against a linebacker.

- Soft post on the inside foot.
- Weight on the shaded area.
- Jam set foot into the ground, with the whole foot on the ground.
- The post foot must not be flat. If the lineman rocks back on the heel of his post foot, he has stepped back too far with his set foot.

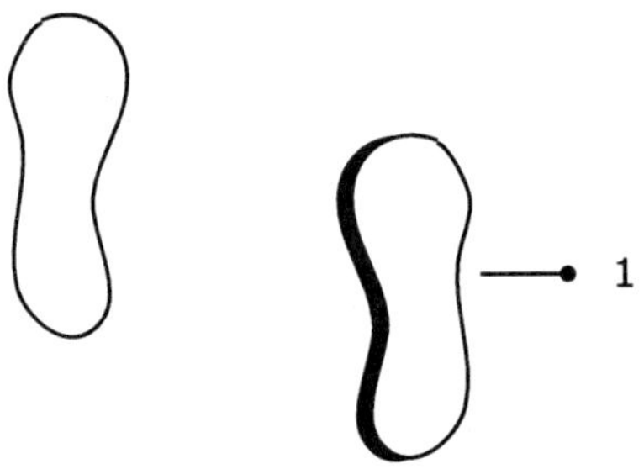

PASS PROTECTION SET VS A 3-TECHNIQUE

- Soft post on the outside foot.
- The set foot vs. a 3-technique should kick back and out, and the whole foot should be placed on the ground. The post foot should stay up and should not be dragged until the lineman reads the target. This will deny any inside movement.

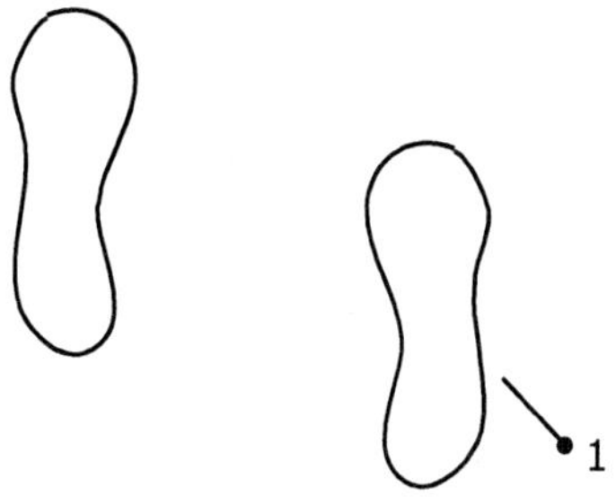

PASS PROTECTION SET VS A LOOSE 3-TECHNIQUE

- Drop set and slide.
- The set foot should move the same vs. a loose 3 as the lineman moved it vs. a tight 3. The difference is that the post foot should drag to a spot to get the lineman back to a stagger, and in a position to time his jam. His feet move according to his target. You must try to maintain the foot stagger as long as possible. The wider the man, the deeper the set foot.

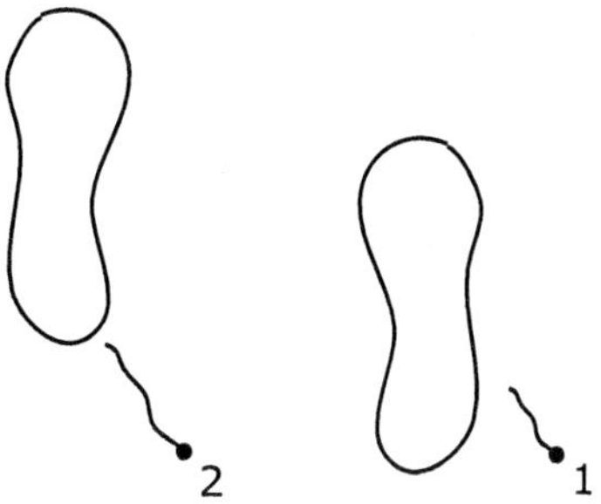

PASS PROTECTION SET VS A LOOSE 5-TECHNIQUE, WHEN ALIGNMENT AND SPEED ARE DIFFICULT

There is an exception to moving the set foot first vs. a loose 5. If the lineman can't get out wide enough to get in the proper position to maintain an inside-out position, then the technique used is the movement of the post foot first. To use this method, he should widen his stance and put his weight on the ball of the set foot. Next, he should take his post foot and bring it over and back in the direction of the set. Then, he should move the set back and over in a normal 5-set. It is important that he doesn't cross over or click his heels together. If this happens, his stance is too narrow. This technique should never be done vs. teams that rush inside with their widest rusher. By using this method, the lineman has widened by half-a-man with two steps, and from that position, he can now continue to work the post, kick stagger.

PASS PROTECTION SET VS A 2i-TECHNIQUE OR A 4i-TECHNIQUE

When blocking a man in either a 2i- or 4i-technique, the lineman's weight must be shifted to his set foot and his first step must come with his post foot. This is especially true when he doesn't have help to the inside. At times, a 2 set will suffice if the defender likes to jump from a 1- to a 2-technique. The lineman should not overstride to the inside. He should try to jam the ball of his post foot into the ground, not his heel. If the defender moves down to the inside, the

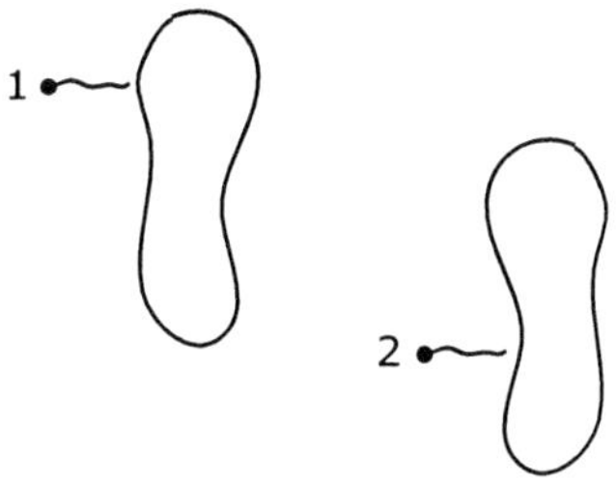

set foot should continue to move in the direction dictated by the target's movement. His knee and toe must deny any inside rush.

STANCE-JAM

The proper set vs. any technique begins with the stance. The lineman should try to pull his weight back in his hips and, at the same time, reach out with his hand without putting very much weight on it. His butt should be slightly up, leaning his weight of his hip over his post foot. This weight distribution, at times, will change vs. other techniques. The initial set is to squat, thrusting his head and shoulders back and driving his chin to his chest, having a bend in his knees, and an arc in the small of his back.

Keeping his shoulders back will help keep him from leaning and tilting at the waist. He must move his feet according to the technique involved and raise his hands up to eye level. He must have palms up and elbows in. Timing the jam is of the utmost importance because if he misfires, he can pop out and lose control of his upper body. He should execute the jam by striking out with his thumbs inside and his palms pushing out. He should try for a full lock out of his arms. The closer the defender, the sooner the jam. If he locks out too soon, he will give the defender something to grab, and the lineman will tend to steer the defender into the quarterback. He will also tend to bail out with his feet. For that reason, he should concentrate on timing the jam. When timing the jam, he should remain in a post-set foot stagger and, as the target moves, so do your feet. He should kick and slide as long as he can to remain staggered. When his man freezes or dances, he should pat the set foot in place, stay staggered, and jam off his post foot. He should not jam off the set foot or lean outside on an outside set. He should always keep his weight over his post-foot hip.

THE CENTER

The center will use the same footwork and all the same alignment techniques as the other linemen. If he has help from a particular guard, he will snuggle set so that his post foot is to the side of his help. (Coaching point: the center should set using his free hand to slow the rusher. This buys him time to get his snapping hand back up as soon as possible.)

ELEMENTS OF THE PASS PROTECTION SET

THE SET. The set pertains to the footwork of the lineman placing him in the proper position vs. the defender's alignment. The set is broken down into the elements of the feet, target, jam, and knee bend.

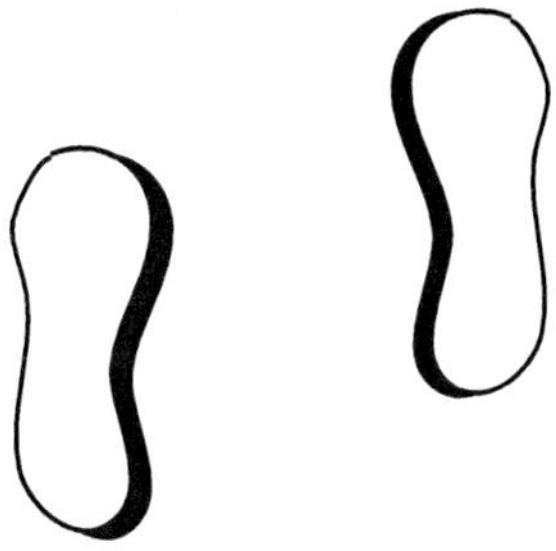

- Post foot. The post foot is the up foot in the pass-blocking stance. The linemen on the right side have their left foot (or post foot) up. The linemen on the left side have their right foot (or post foot) up. The center is balanced in his stance and will determine his post foot at the snap of the ball. His weight is mostly over the hip of his post foot, on the ball of that foot so that the other foot can kick. The knee of his post foot should be angled so he can stay low and lean over in a lateral direction.
- Kick foot. The set foot is the back foot of the stance. In most cases, it is the first foot to move in the stance when set. This gives the lineman the balance and power when he moves to jam. At the set, the whole foot should plant into the ground and the lineman should reach his target from there. If the lineman is heavy on the ball of the set foot, he will lean outside and be caught in a poor balance situation.
- Target. On all blocks, run or pass plays, the lineman must have a target. This will enable the blocker to maintain an inside-out position at all times, keeping the defender from the quarterback. The blocker must maintain his focus on his target throughout the jam process. The lineman should take a specific part of the player's jersey and use it as a bull's eye. For example, a lineman on the left side will pick a spot on the inside of the defender's jersey at the top of the number. The use of such a small target will allow the blocker to concentrate on the inside half of the man, instead of going for head fakes or false movements of the defender's shoulders, etc. A lineman must never honor an outside fake and should always honor an inside fake. He should never get beat inside.

Left side: The lineman's target is the small top of #6
Right side: The lineman's target is the small top of #5

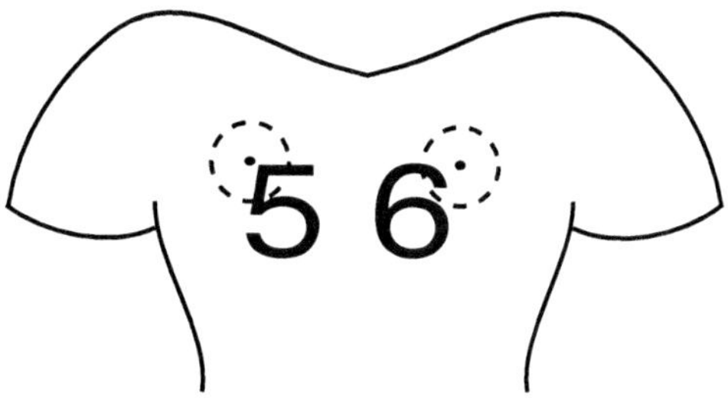

- Knee bend. The lineman should stay in a duck position, which involves a natural knee bend. If a lineman is 6'6", he shouldn't be expected to squat down to 5'6". But during a blocking progression, contact, and movement, he should have power-producing angles in his knees. His stagger-post, set foot should cause him to squat. When he squats, he should have an arc in the small of his back. He should use the same posture as when he is doing a power clean with his shin in and shoulders back which keeps his neck bulled. If his head tilts down, his body will follow. He should keep his face clean and out of the jam.

CHAPTER 37

GENERAL LINE PASS TERMINOLOGY

Key:
OLM = offensive lineman
PSG = playside guard
PST = playside tackle
DLM = defensive lineman
BSG = backside guard
BST = backside tackle

COVERED Call used to indicate that a defensive lineman is head-up or shaded on the LOS.	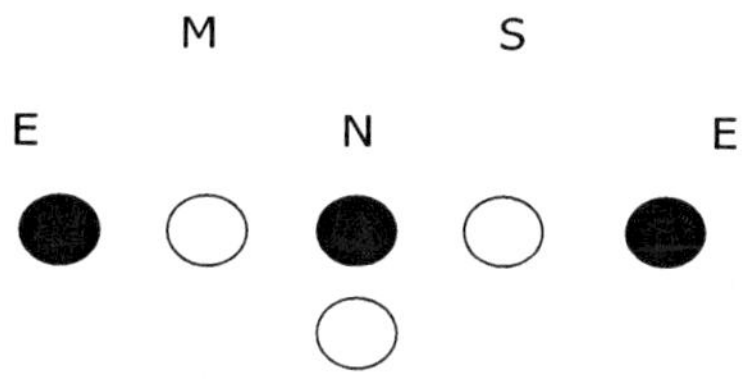
UNCOVERED Call used to indicate when no defensive lineman is head-up in a 3-or 2-point stance on the LOS.	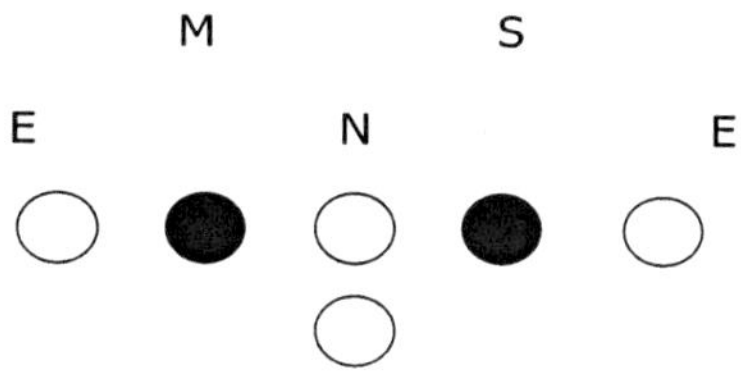
QUICK SET An aggressive, show pass movement on the LOS.	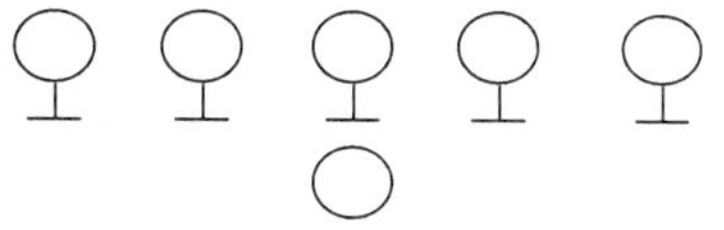

BOB

Call made by the PST to alert the PSG to block #1 on the LOS and the PST to block #2 on the LOS (big-on-big).

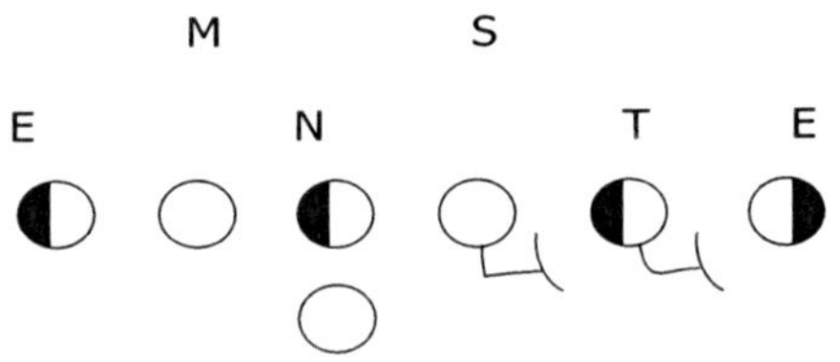

UP/DOWN

Call made by the center to determine if the protection is to be executed from a 2-point or a 3-point stance.

ELEPHANT

Call in which the entire offensive line track zones their playside gap, selling the run, allowing no leakage.

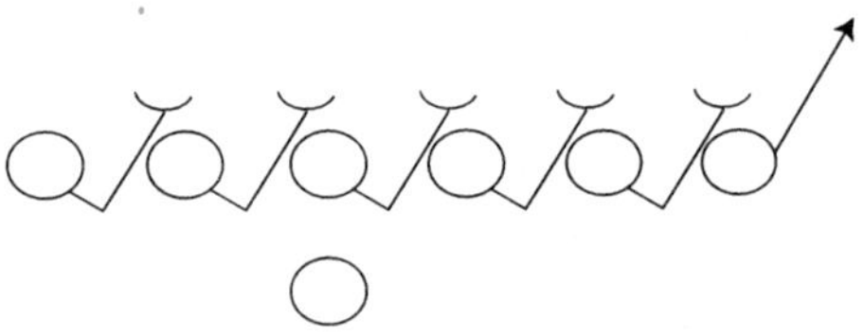

RAIDER

A frontside protection call vs. overhang which directs the PST to block man on, and the running back to block overhang call side.

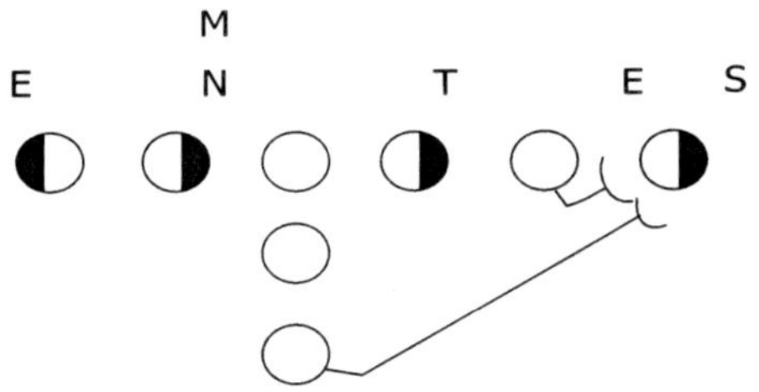

BANDIT

A backside protection call vs. overhang which alerts the running back and the uncovered OLM of a possible stunt or dog situation backside.

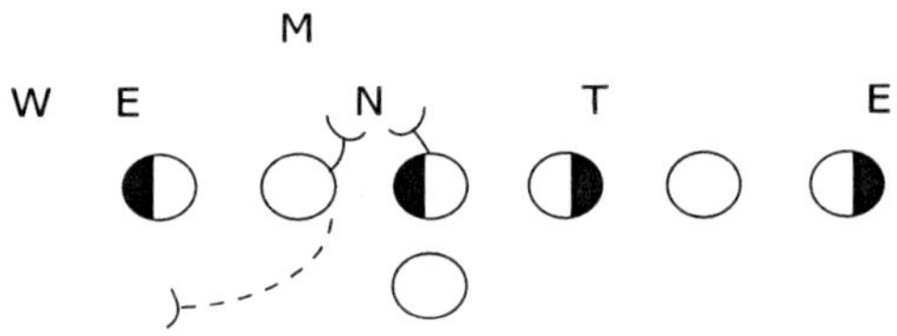

BAT

A frontside protection call vs. a B-gap linebacker threat. The PST and running back exchange assignments. The PST blocks the B-gap threat; the running back blocks the PST's man.

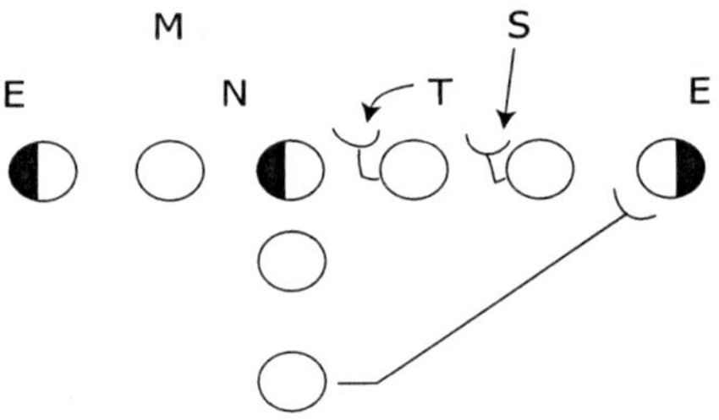

TAG

A frontside protection call vs. an A-gap, linebacker threat. The PSG and PST exchange assignments. The PSG blocks the A-gap threat; the PST blocks B-gap threat.

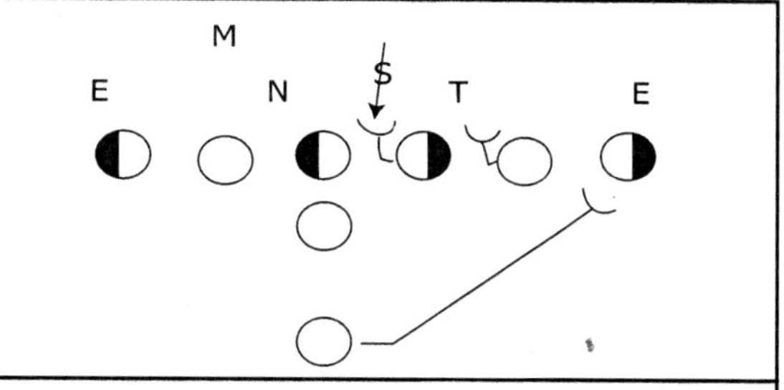

JOKER

Call by the right guard which directs the center to the right to handle A- and B-gap threats to the right side of the protection. The right guard and the center combo on the down lineman to the linebacker.

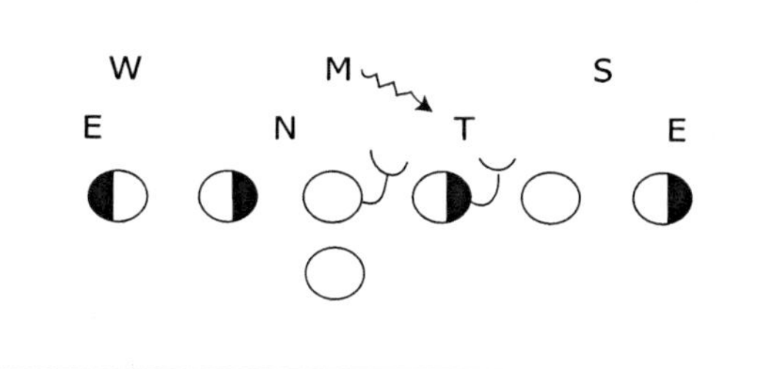

CLOWN

Call by the left guard which directs the center to the left to handle A- and B-gap threats to the left side of the protection. The left guard and the center combo on the down defender to the linebacker.

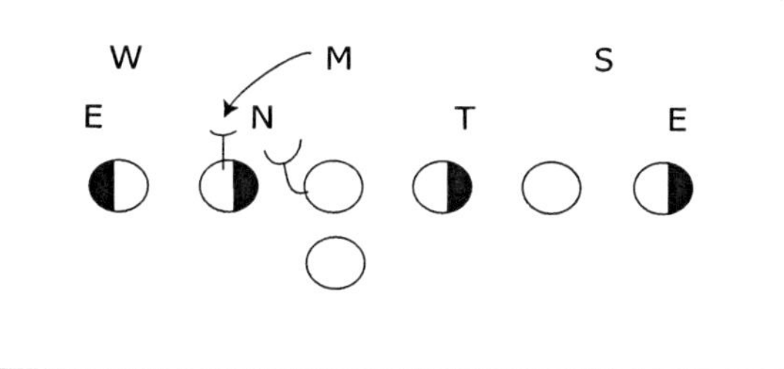

GHOST

Call made by the PST or PSG when sugar linebackers bail out on pre-snap. Ghost call cancels previous calls made to handle linebacker blitzes. Everyone returns to base rules of protection called.

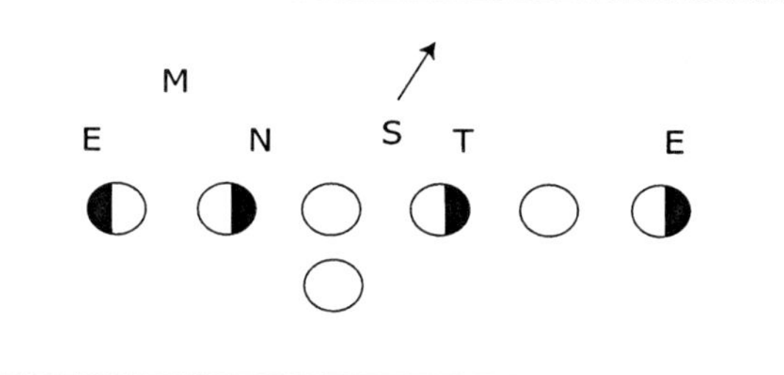

WIDE

Call made by the BST when covered, and overhang outside. Alerts PSG and center to get depth and width to block widest defender to their backside gap.

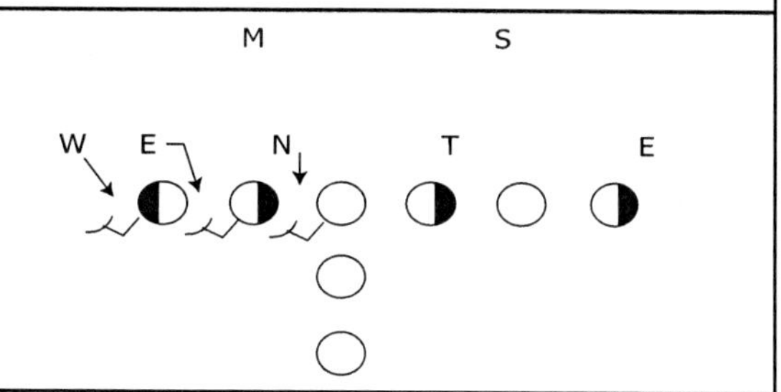

SQUEEZE

A backside protection call by either BSG/ BST vs. A- or B-gap linebacker threat. The BSG blocks A-gap threat; BST blocks the B-gap threat. (vs. Eagle and DBL Eagle fronts only.)

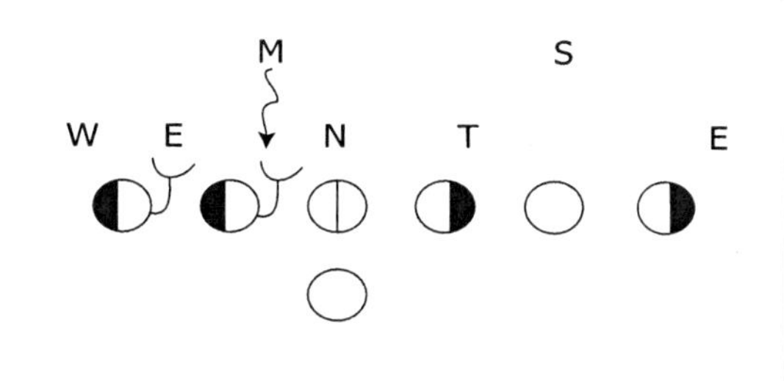

<table>
<tr><td>FAN

Call made by the BST, when covered plus one defender outside. Alerts the BSG to block #1 on the LOS and the BST to block #2 on the LOS.</td><td>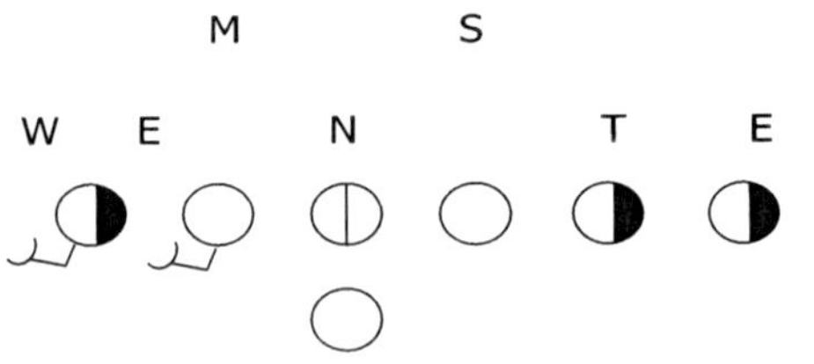</td></tr>
<tr><td>DUAL READ

Technique used by an uncovered lineman where he scans his assignment on the second level, and then works backside to pick up the free rusher.</td><td>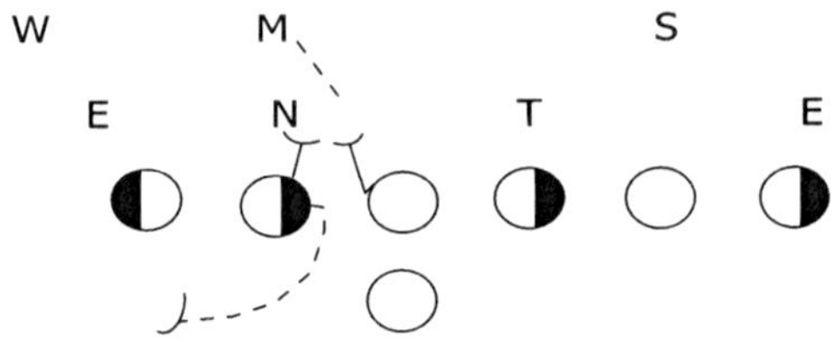</td></tr>
<tr><td>DROP SET

A show-pass-first movement, working for depth off the LOS.</td><td>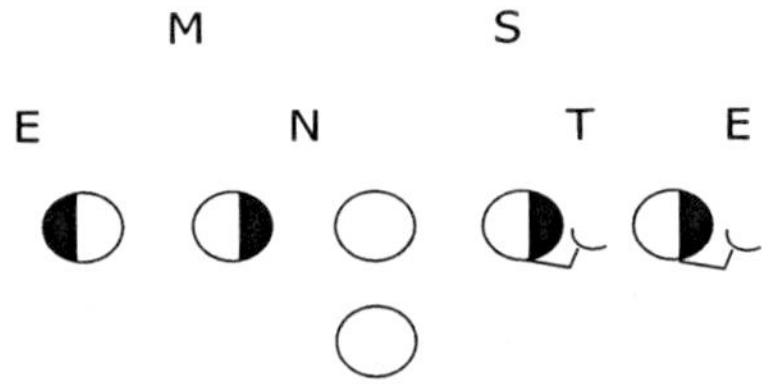</td></tr>
<tr><td>SOLID

Call made to alert everyone to block the man on vs. Eagle or DBL Eagle fronts.</td><td>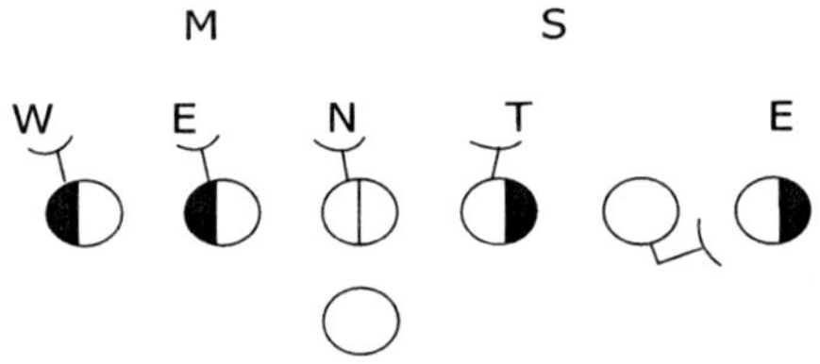</td></tr>
<tr><td>KICK ANGLE

Technique used by tackles, kicking for depth and width with their outside foot and sliding their inside foot back to a base post set. (Used by a wide rusher, or to widen a rusher's rush lane.)</td><td>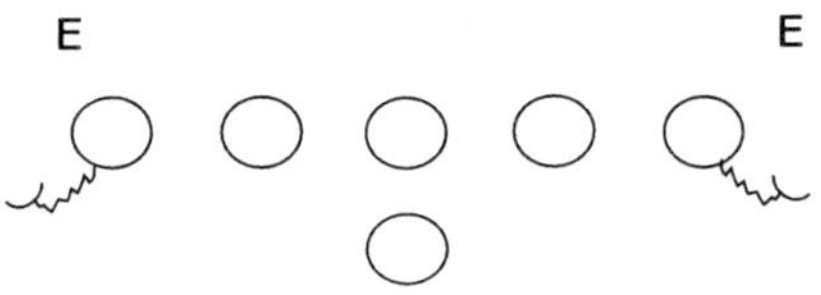</td></tr>
<tr><td>LOCK

Technique used by the BST on naked and boot protection vs. overhang. The BST locks on man, shutting down backside B-gap threat.</td><td>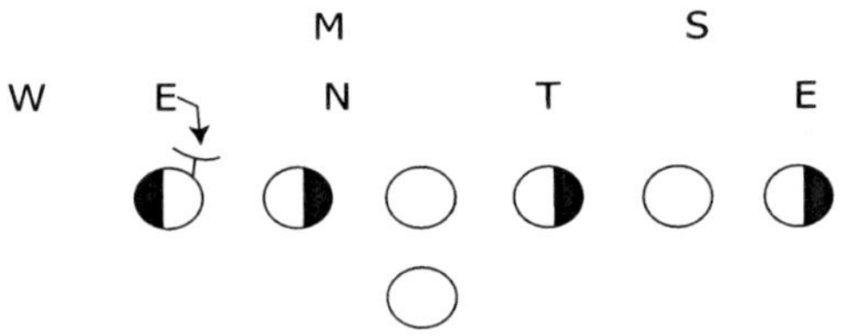</td></tr>
</table>

JUMP CUT Technique used by the PST on screens. The PST aggressive sets and jump cuts the end man on the LOS outside thigh board.	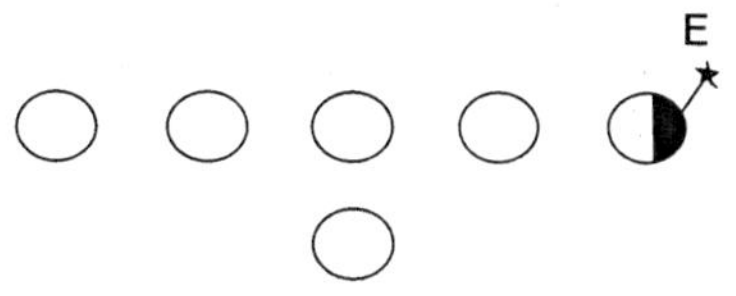
BOOT PULL Pulling technique in which the guard pulls down the LOS and reads the DE. Vs. no color upfield = log DE. Vs. color upfield = cut/log the DE.	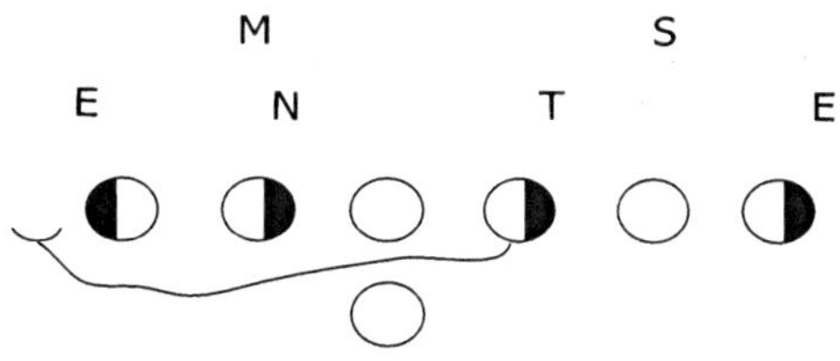
CLIMB Technique used by the uncovered OLM. Sets quickly, selling pass, and then climbs to second-level linebacker.	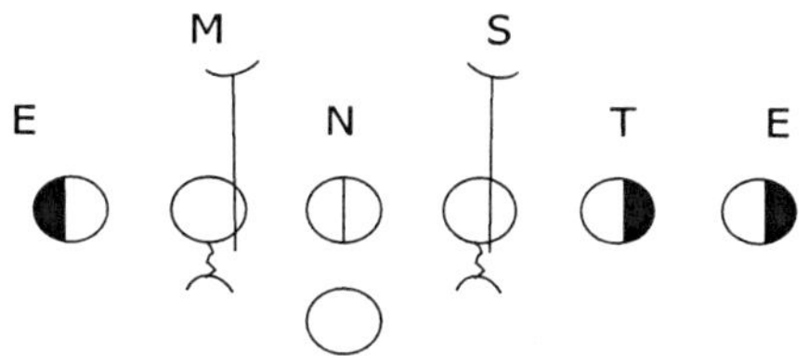

CHAPTER 38

PASS-PROTECTION DRILLS

Each drill requires the offensive lineman to use good feet, base, leverage and hand techniques. The key is to progress to live situations, but first allow the lineman to realize success and develop confidence in his techniques, including the following:

- Set Position. The lineman sets up over a wide base, with the inside foot is up and his outside foot is staggered. His feet are flat on the ground, with his toes slightly turned outward. The weight is centered between the insteps of the feet, with knees bent and tailed arched. The hands are up, carrying them out in front, about six inches short of full extension, with the shoulders back.
- Quick Set. Lineman assumes 3-point stance, with a partner facing them. On coach's command, lineman quick sets as their partner tries to grab the back of the lineman's head. The emphasis is to set quickly and get their heads, shoulders, back, and hands up as fast as possible, without being grabbed.
- Sets by Alignment:
  - √ Head up. Soft post with the inside foot. A lateral step, keeping the weight centered between the feet. This is a one-step set, and then react.
  - √ Inside Shade. Hard post with the inside foot, shuffling inside with the shoulders staying square. Cover the defender nose-to-nose and toes-to-toes.
  - √ Tight shade. Soft post with the outside foot. A lateral step, keeping the weight centered between the feet. This is a one-step, set, and then react.
  - √ Outside shade. Drop-set with the outside foot and slide the inside foot straight back. The shoulders stay square. It is important to gain a little depth and width on this set.

√ Wide shade Kick angle set with the outside foot and slide the inside foot, gaining depth and width. The shoulders are square, and the inside foot is pointed straight ahead. It is important not to keep drifting. If the rusher is in front of the lineman, he should give up the inside. As the rusher works outside, he should continue to kick angle and slide with inside leverage, forcing the rusher to stay outside.

A number of drills can be performed to develop the skills and techniques that are involved in pass protections, including the following:

- Lateral Wave Drill. The lineman works from either a 2- or 3-point stance. On command, the lineman sets, shuffles, and punches vs. air in the direction given. The emphasis is on developing foot quickness, redirection, and body control.
- Form Punch Drill. vs. a bag or a sled, the lineman aligns in a 2- or 3-point stance with with defender in striking distance. On the coach's command, the lineman strikes up and out with a punch. Initially the drill is performed slowly and the gradually works to full speed. The emphasis is on timing the initial punch and the proper hand placement in the defender's framework.
- Punch Drills. vs. a bag or a sled, the lineman assumes 2-point set position and works on his hand-eye coordination by performing various punch drills, for example:

  √ 2-Hand punch – 10 reps

  √ 1-Hand punch – 10 reps RT hand, 10 LT hand

  √ 1-Hand combinations – RT/LT – 10 reps

  √ 1-Hand combinations – RT high/LT low, LT high/RT low – 10 reps

  √ 2-Hand opposite corner – RT/ LT – 10 reps

  √ 1-Hand cross punch – RT/LT – 10 reps

  √ 2-Hand punches vs. spin – chest, shoulder, back, shoulder

  √ Blind punch – With eyes closed, reset hands and punch as partner slaps hand down. (Hands stay tight as they are reset.)
- Pound the Post Drill. Against bags or a sled, the lineman power shuffles down the line and punches the target. The sequence of the punches is as follows — first, a 1-hand punch RT/LT, then 1-2 alternate punch combos RT/LT, and finally, a 2-hand punch. The emphasis is on maintaining balance and body control while covering up the target and timing the punch.
- Kick Angle Post Drill. Against three bags set on 45-degree angles. The lineman works at a kick angle, steps and punches the target as the rushers work upfield. The emphasis is on maintaining the angle with his shoulders square, timing the punch, and maintaining an inside position on the defender.

- Mirror Drill. The lineman assumes a 2-point set position, hands behind his back, with a partner across from him. The rusher works, using lateral movements. The lineman shuffles, leading with the foot in the direction of the rusher, moving his whole body as he travels. The emphasis is to not lean and to not chop his feet. The lineman must keep both of his feet planted in the ground with his shoulders back, maintaining body control.
- Zig Zag Drill. The lineman assumes a 2-point set position with a partner across from him. Lineman mirrors and reacts to the rusher's movement. When the rusher goes inside, the lineman should hand post his inside foot and shuffle as he punches. When the rusher works outside, he should kick angle and slide, and then punch. The emphasis is on using proper footwork vs. movement and shutting down the rusher, thereby making him redirect.
- Push Pull Drill. The drill involves working in pairs, on acting as a blocker while the other serves as a rusher. The lineman assumes a 2-point set position. The rusher grabs the lineman's shoulders and tries to push, pull, and twist him off balance. The lineman fights to maintain balance and body control by sitting and gathering his feet.
- Punch-Separate Drill. The drill involves working in pairs, similar to the previous drill. The lineman assumes a 3-point stance across from the rusher with a bag. On command, the rusher walks forward into the lineman. The lineman strikes his punch, and then separates from the rusher. He then recovers and strikes again.
- Blood Drill. Three rushers align in a straight, lateral line with bags. They stand shoulder-to-shoulder, with a lineman set in front of the middle rusher. On command, the lineman sets in a 2-point set position. As the coach points to defender, the rusher comes straight ahead. The lineman reacts to what he sees. If he is sent against the outside rusher, he will always return to the middle after he punches and separates from the rusher, making him ready for the next rusher.
- Machine Gun Drill. Three rushers align in a single file behind each other. A lineman assumes a 3-point stance. On command, the lineman sets and takes on the first rusher and separates. The next two rushers side rush, one to the left, the other to the right. The emphasis is on developing reaction time, timing of the punch, and separating and shuffling to cover up the rusher.
- Square Drill. The lineman assumes his 2-point set position. Four defenders with shields box him in, one in front, one behind, and one on each side of him. On command, the lineman is given directional turns (RT/LT). The lineman turns to the bag and two-hand punches the shield he is facing. The emphasis is to react, cover the rusher up, time the punch, and keep the hands up.
- Bull Rush Drill. The lineman assumes a 2-point set position. Hugging a bag, the rusher comes straight upfield into the lineman. The lineman quickly punches and locks his hands on the defender, and then flops backward with his feet bracing the rusher's charge. The emphasis is on a delivering a blow quickly and then resetting and flopping the feet and weight backwards.

- Twist Drill. The lineman assumes a 3-point stance with three defenders aligned opposite him. The two outside defenders are holding shields. On command, the lineman sets as the defender over him executes a loop outside to his right or left. The outside defender penetrates hard inside. The lineman drop- sets his foot in the direction of the looper, attacks the penetrator, and turns it into run blocking, yelling, "switch!" The emphasis is on reacting to looper and attacking the slanter, covering him up.

- Twist Pick Up Drill. Two lineman align in a 3-point stance with two defenders aligned across from them. On command, the lineman set and react to the two defenders. One defender will loop, and the other will penetrate. The lineman covering the "looper" drop-sets in the direction of the defensive looper, attacks the penetrating defender, and turns it into a run block as he yells, "switch". The "drive man" stretches the penetrating defender to the looper. When he gets bumped off, he gets depth to pick up the looping defender, either two-hand framing him, or cut blocking him.

- Jump Set Drill. This technique is used when the lineman quick sets and jumps the rusher quickly. It is used only vs. an outside-shaded defender. The lineman takes a drop-step with his outside foot and places his inside foot at the same point. He then attacks forward, jamming and locking on the rusher's chest as he walks into him.

- Spin Drill. The lineman assumes a 3-point stance, while the rusher aligns in any shade. On command, the lineman quick sets and delivers the initial punch; then the rusher goes into a series of spin moves. The lineman must separate from the rusher and use his hands to pass the spin. The emphasis is to have live hands on the rusher's back and hand-over-hand placement when working the shoulder of the rusher. While utilizing good footwork, the blocker should keep his body squared up on the rusher.

- One-on-One Drill. Five linemen set up with five rushers across from them. The coach stands behind the linemen and points at one rusher, who will rush upfield. On the coach's command, all five lineman work sets by the alignment of the rusher. One lineman takes on the rusher, while the others work on pass sets. The emphasis is to work on sets vs. alignment by setting quickly, ready for combat. The rusher is changed on each snap.

- Two-on-Two Drill. The rusher executes a straight rush or a twist. The linemen work together to pick up man protection or zone twist pick-ups.

- Full Line Schemes Drill. The lineman align on the LOS, with the down defenders and the linebackers aligned across from them. The coach stands behind the linemen with scripted protections to review. Linemen assume their proper splits, levels, and alignments of the protection given. On the coach's command, the unit picks up their protection assignment. (Coaching point: work all base protections, and then incorporate twist, dogs, and blitzes.)

ABOUT THE AUTHOR

Harold Etheridge is the offensive line coach at the United States Military Academy at West Point. Prior to assuming his present position in 2000, he served in the same capacity at Illinois State University (Normal, Illinois). During his tenure on the Redbirds' staff, he tutored four All-American performers and five first-team, All-Gateway Conference honorees. In addition, the Redbirds established school standards in both rushing offense and passing offense. He played a major role in helping to develop an offense that virtually rewrote the school's record book, molding a high-powered attack that ranked among the nation's best.

A 1981 graduate of Western New Mexico University, Etheridge was a three-time all-conference pick at offensive guard and was invited to tryouts with a trio of National Football League clubs upon graduation. From 1983-88, he then spent five years coaching at the high school level, serving stints at both Gallup H.S. in New Mexico and Ballard H.S. in Kentucky. Subsequently, he accepted an assistant coaching position at the University of Kentucky. Following a three-year tour on the coaching sidelines in Lexington (1988-90), Etheridge joined the staff at Illinois State in 1991. He is widely regarded as an exceptional teacher of offensive line fundamentals and techniques.

The Gallup, N.M., native and his wife, Jeanne, are the parents of 4-year old twins, Clayton and Eliza. The family resides at West Point.